# The Journey of a Woman

# $\mathcal{T}$HE

# $\mathcal{J}$OURNEY OF

# A $\mathcal{W}$OMAN

## JANE HANSEN

### Regal

A Division of Gospel Light
Ventura, California, U.S.A.

Published by Regal Books
A Division of Gospel Light
Ventura, California, U.S.A.
Printed in U.S.A.

Regal Books is a ministry of Gospel Light, an evangelical Christian publisher dedicated to serving the local church. We believe God's vision for Gospel Light is to provide church leaders with biblical, user-friendly materials that will help them evangelize, disciple and minister to children, youth and families.

It is our prayer that this Regal book will help you discover biblical truth for your own life and help you meet the needs of others. May God richly bless you.

For a free catalog of resources from Regal Books and Gospel Light please call your Christian supplier, or contact us at 1-800-4-GOSPEL or at www.gospellight.com.

Cover Design by Barbara LeVan Fisher
Interior Design by Britt Rocchio
Edited by David Webb

**Library of Congress Cataloging-in-Publication Data**
Hansen, Jane.
    The journey of a woman / Jane Hansen.
        p.    cm.
    Includes bibliographical references.
    ISBN 0-8307-2362-5  (hardcover).
    1. Hansen, Jane.   2.  Christian biography — United States.      I. Title.
        BR1725.H236A3          1998
        269'.2'092—dc21                                                              98-34360
        [B]                                                                                  CIP

1 2 3 4 5 6 7 8 9 10 11 12 13 14 15 16 17 18 19 20 / 04 03 02 01 00 99 98

Rights for publishing this book in other languages are contracted by Gospel Literature International (GLINT). GLINT also provides technical help for the adaptation, translation and publishing of Bible study resources and books in scores of languages worldwide. For further information, write to GLINT at P.O. Box 4060, Ontario, CA 91761-1003, U.S.A. You may also send e-mail to Glintint@aol.com, or visit their web site at www.glint.org.

THIS BOOK IS DEDICATED TO MY

DEAR HUSBAND HOWARD, WHO HAS WALKED

WITH ME ON THE JOURNEY TO LOVE.

# $\mathscr{C}$ONTENTS

FOREWORD BY DICK AND MARILYN WILLIAMSON      9

FOREWORD BY HOWARD HANSEN      11

ACKNOWLEDGMENTS      13

INTRODUCTION      15

chapter 1    PAIN IN THE LITTLE RED HOUSE      17

chapter 2    THE FAMILY TREE      29

chapter 3    MAKING CHOICES      43

chapter 4    TO CALIFORNIA WITH A PROMISE      59

chapter 5    A NEW DIMENSION      67

chapter 6    GOING FOR THE HEART      87

chapter 7    THIRSTY PILGRIMS      105

chapter 8    OUT OF HIDING      123

chapter 9    THE FACE OF FORGIVENESS      143

chapter 10    MERCY TRIUMPHS      161

chapter 11    THE JOURNEY TO LOVE      175

EPILOGUE      197

ENDNOTES      199

# FOREWORD

"GIVE HER OF THE FRUIT OF HER HANDS;
AND LET HER OWN WORKS PRAISE
HER IN THE GATES."

PROVERBS 31:31, *KJV*

We have been privileged to be Jane's friends and have watched the changes in her life as the Lord ministered words of faith, truth and encouragement to her. We have seen the person God created her to be coming forth. This happened as she gave up the protection of the "person" she had been using to cover up what she saw as her inadequacies.

We believe that Jesus used the Holy Spirit to uncover the inside woman of Jane Hansen so that she could become an able minister to others as president of Aglow International.

Vulnerability means to be "open to be wounded"—no self-protection. Jane has risked this, letting you see her heart, being transparent before you in order to help you. She believes that what leaves the heart reaches the heart.

We believe that Jane's desire for you as you read this book is that you take it into your heart for your help.

DICK AND MARILYN WILLIAMSON

# FOREWORD

I took Jane to the airport early this morning. She was off on one of many weekends of speaking to groups of ladies throughout the United States and overseas.

She called me this evening from Dallas, Texas. Because of an intense storm, the flight had been redirected, finally arriving at Dallas/Fort Worth Airport after a five-hour delay. She would not arrive at her final destination until after midnight. She asked me to pray for her so she would have peace and rest. I did.

This evening I drove to downtown Edmonds, parked the car and took a walk on the lovely street along Puget Sound. It was windless, the water was calm, and the sun was beginning to set. A balmy evening. Beautiful. At the end of the street I sat on a bench and took in the view that both Jane and I admire so much. I felt lonely; I wished Jane were there with me. Yet I knew she was doing God's will as a speaker and teacher.

As I sat there in peace and quiet, tears came to my eyes. I felt sad, yet it was a good feeling because I felt love, not only for Jane, but also for the Father. I can now feel love and show emotion. It hasn't always been like that. But now I have a Father I can talk with anytime.

I now have the love of Jesus in my heart. I can now have tears in my eyes and experience emotion. I can now have feelings. I can now forgive and be forgiven. I can now have peace in my life.

Jane was traveling, yet I felt her near me, and I thanked God for her and the help she has given me through these years. Had I not married Jane, I would never have been in the place I am now. God has been good to Jane and me.

Jane has a heart for all people. She is a giving, generous and caring person. What she has written in this book has taken many hours of burning the midnight oil so that what is said will help someone out there who reads it. What was written is the truth, and I admire her for telling the whole story.

I thank God for Dick and Marilyn Williamson and their love, understanding and friendship. Their help to Jane and me has been life changing.

I honor Jane today with a heart full of love for her.

Thank you, Jane, for putting up with me and a lot of bad behavior during these many years. Thanks for your understanding and, most of all, thanks for your undying love for me through it all. You are a great lady.

May God bless you always. I love you very, very much.

YOUR HUSBAND, HOWARD

# $\mathscr{A}$CKNOWLEDGMENTS

Although this is the story of one woman, it could never have been written without the love and encouragement of many, many people.

Two people head the list—my former pastor and his wife, Dick and Marilyn Williamson. I will be eternally grateful for the love, counsel and truth they have so faithfully imparted to me.

God used them to bring me out of myself, out of my hiddenness, out of my pain and into the light of His truth. The help I received through their biblical counseling has been nothing less than the radical, life-giving heart surgery that is crucial to having a changed heart.

I am especially filled with gratitude as I think of my husband, Howard. His support and belief in me—and in this book—has never faltered. Without his willingness to be known and his desire to help others, this story could not have been told. It is a great tribute to the work of God in his life.

I am also grateful for my wonderful family, Jeff, Lisa and Scott. Their love and support continue to be great sources of strength and encouragement.

It is not easy to feel another person's feelings, hear her heart and then communicate that message to others. My friend, Carol Greenwood, has done just that in this book. Her faithfulness and commitment have helped make *The Journey of a Woman* a reality.

No one writes a book alone. Karen Anderson and JoAnne Sekowsky gave invaluable editorial assistance. So many others cheered me on with their prayers, support and varied practical help in time of need: Ardis Benson, Lorene Carlson, Doris Eaker, Diane Fink, Pat Gaines, Susan Goodnight, Cheryl Morgan, Christa Murrow, Betty Ringer, and Deena Wilson.

As I reflect on all these precious, godly people the Lord has so lovingly placed in my life to walk alongside me, I am truly humbled and blessed.

*JANE HANSEN*

Edmonds, Washington, U.S.A.
Easter 1998

# $\mathcal{I}$NTRODUCTION

I love the way God's Word so clearly shows life as it was *really* lived by those He came to save. It's all there: the good and the bad, the mountaintops and the valleys, the triumphs and the failures—the truth of the process. Their struggles and their victories encourage us onward in our own journey through life.

The pain of God's people was not hidden, nor were their fears or insecurities covered over. God is so willing to let it all be seen, that we may be encouraged and helped toward fulfilling His purpose for our lives.

Writing this book has not been easy for me. I have struggled with the fear of being known. Yet because of the help I have received, I feel that my struggles and victories might also encourage you on your journey.

In his book *Inside Out*, Dr. Larry Crabb states, "The church needs leaders who can involve themselves in other people's lives with the joy of integrity and transparency...willing to be deeply known for the sake of helping others."[1]

He goes on to say, "God wants to change good disciples into powerfully loving servants who leave an indelible mark on people they touch."[2]

This is my prayer: that my life, all of it, can somehow touch your life, and together we can walk that journey toward love. This would fulfill the prayer of Jesus that the world would see our love and come to know the Father.

# $\mathcal{P}$AIN IN THE $\mathcal{L}$ITTLE $\mathcal{R}$ED $\mathcal{H}$OUSE

The real estate agent eased his car to a stop alongside the white picket fence. "Well, folks, here we are. The second house on our list today, and is it ever a charmer." It was the fall of 1959 and my husband, Howard, and I were hunting for our first house in a neighborhood close to what is now Seattle's Northgate Mall.

The agent placed his left arm on the steering wheel as he turned toward Howard and said with man-to-man intimacy, "Your wife's going to love this little dollhouse." As he spoke, he rolled his eyes as if to say he understood the mystery of a woman's tastes. Then, glancing toward me in the back seat, he resumed his professional demeanor. "Mrs. Hansen, ahh...would you mind if I just called you 'Jane'?"

I don't remember answering him. My mind was not on the formalities of agent/client protocol as I stood transfixed by the sight in front of me. I was speechless.

Inside a little white gate and up a short walk, stood my picture-perfect house—the kind I'd yearned for ever since I was a preacher's kid growing up in church parsonages.

Amazingly, this little red house looked like a double of a favorite house from my childhood that we passed by every Sunday on our way to church in Akron, Ohio. I was bathed in nostalgia as I stared at it. I had found a long lost friend.

"This little gem just came on the market, Jane." The real estate agent grinned at me, then turned back to open the car door. "Come on folks, let's take the grand tour." He slid out and slammed his door behind him.

Before Howard could open the passenger door, I leaned forward, put my hand on his shoulder and blurted, "Howie, it does look good." Howard nodded as he carefully swung three-year-old Jeff from his lap onto the parking strip. He reached back to help me out, then boosted the excited tot up high on his broad shoulders. I felt a surge of pride; I loved the natural way Howard took charge of his little family.

We followed the Realtor through the gate and up the walk as he continued his patter. "You and Howard are wise to get settled before your baby comes. There's probably not a better home in the north end for your little family. This one has two bedrooms, big kitchen, nice fireplace and a family room for the kids." He paused on the doorstep, looking for some kind of response from me, but I was still too excited to say anything.

We walked into the living room and the men stopped in front of the fireplace. The Realtor brushed his hand across the mirror work above the fireplace. "Take a look at this craftsmanship, Howard. You rarely see that quality work anymore." Howard gently eased Jeff off his shoulders and onto the floor as I wandered off to explore the rest of the house.

The Realtor's voice followed me, "Wait till you see the apple tree in the backyard, Jane." I heard the men resume their conversation, but all I could think about was decorating this house.

It would be the first chance in my life to choose paint colors, wallpaper and furniture.

Jeff and I found the bedrooms and opened closet doors. As we walked down the hall, I talked to my towheaded son as if he were my decorating consultant. "Let's see, honey, I'll use lavender and white in Mommy and Daddy's room, repaint the little bedroom for you and our new baby, and hang white curtains and green towels in the bathroom.

"New baby can sleep with me, Mommy," Jeff offered as he flashed an innocent smile. "I take care of him." Wrinkling his freckled nose, he was an irresistible target for a motherly kiss.

"Do you have any idea how much I love you, honey?" I leaned over impulsively and put my lips against his upturned cheek. Straightening up, I wrapped my hand around his little one and walked him toward the kitchen.

Jeff scooted ahead, but I paused under the archway to the kitchen. Looking in at this inviting room and out to the garden beyond the large windows was like being tossed into a fresh spring morning ablaze with color and reverberating with the music of my favorite symphony. A rush of energy flooded me as all of my senses engaged at once.

I felt exhilarated. The sensation of the new life flutter-kicking within me only enhanced the wonderful sense of expectancy rising within me.

*I could bloom in a place like this*, I thought. *This is what I've always longed for, a home of my own.*

## A New Start

At that moment, I could not have told you why I felt such a need for a new start in a new place. My longing for my own home was the immediate answer but, as I would discover later, my yearning went way beyond satisfying my life's desire to be a homemaker.

The apartment we lived in on Queen Anne Hill was certainly not undesirable. But I wanted to feel the freedom of ownership. I wanted to turn loose all my creative homemaking energy to personalize our surroundings. Decorating, painting, sewing—I loved creating warm, inviting rooms.

"Mommy, look at the little doors!" Jeff's voice brought me back from my reverie, but before I could react, he ran to my side. When his pudgy fingers tugged at my skirt, I couldn't resist his enthusiasm. Together we ran to the long row of cupboards under the counter and I squatted down with him. We giggled as we took turns opening and shutting each door.

As the afternoon sun splashed through the large windows, diffusing warmth and light throughout the room, this joy-filled moment between mother and son struck me as heaven sent.

"Your wife like to bake?" It was as if the Realtor read my mind as he ushered Howard into the kitchen. I had just mentally baked an apple pie using apples from the backyard tree.

"Yeah, Jane's a great cook," Howard responded matter-of-factly.

While they talked, I fingered the long, white counter tops, my creative juices flowing.

Finally, I couldn't contain myself. My words tumbled out as I broke into their discussion. "Howie, can't you just see this kitchen with red checkered curtains? I can sew them in a snap. It won't cost much to buy a red canister set and it will really pull this room together, don't you think?"

The agent laughed at my outburst as Howard answered, "Sure, whatever you want to do." I watched my husband walk toward the door and head out to inspect the backyard, then I followed him. I stopped immediately, however, catching my breath at what I saw. The backyard looked like a park. It was ablaze with watermelon-colored poppies and flower beds exploding with color. Surrounded by the white picket fence, complete with apple tree as advertised, the sight was far more beautiful than I glimpsed through the window.

Years later, I would drive by this home again and see only a small, nondescript house on a quiet street, but then—at that moment—standing close to Howard, it felt like a mansion to me.

The Realtor cleared his throat in the silence. "I think your wife's found her dream house, Howard." Eager to close the sale, he began to turn back into the house. "Why don't we all head over to my office, have some coffee and talk about making an offer?"

Before Howard could move, I grabbed his hand and squeezed it hard. "It's perfect, Howie." Howard stood silent for a moment and I barely breathed.

"Let's do it," he said. And we did.

We bought the little red house that sunny, blue-sky Seattle day. Within six weeks, we moved into our first home.

## Imperfect Reality

Perfect. Perfect. Perfect. The words sang in my heart like a lullaby during those early nights in the red house. I'd lie in bed next to Howard, mentally rocking myself to sleep with my perpetual fantasy: Life will be perfect for our little family with this dream home to wrap around them. I could almost hear the bluebirds of happiness chirping out reservations for nest space in our apple tree.

However, within weeks of moving in, I wondered if the bluebirds had migrated south. What was wrong? I had everything I wanted. I should be happy. But happiness did not move in with our furniture and boxes as I thought it would. In fact, something else was creeping in like an unwelcome fog around the edges of my heart as I sewed curtains and painted bedrooms.

## Happiness Is...

It may be hard to believe from the perspective of today's fast-paced, success-oriented society, but in those years, I wasn't interested in pursuing a career, prestige or financial success. In fact, it never occurred to me.

I'd been raised in a pastor's modest home in the Midwest, and my aspirations reflected the simple, down-to-earth, growing-up days of the '40s and '50s. Anytime anyone asked me what I wanted out of life, I gave them my standard answer: "Give me a home, children and a husband who loves me, and I'll live happily ever after."

I BELIEVE IT IS A GOD-GIVEN DESIRE
IN A WOMAN TO FASHION A HOME AND
TO LOVINGLY FILL IT WITH WARMTH
AND BEAUTY. UNDERSTANDABLY, MY
HOPES FOR OUR LIFE IN THE LITTLE
RED HOUSE WERE HIGH.

I came by this love of home and hearth naturally. I remember as a little girl of four or five, stepping onto the yellow linoleum floor of my great-grandmother's kitchen in rural Ohio, closing my eyes and inhaling the intoxicating aroma of whole wheat bread baking in the oven.

Later, as I watched her bend over her sideboard to roll out pie crust, it was as if everything in that cozy kitchen sang out, "Home is wonderful. It is warm, secure and safe."

My mother followed in this homemaking tradition. In every parsonage we called home, she plunged in to shape a comfortable, attractive haven for our family. Her creativity seemed inexhaustible—even in some of the more aesthetically challenging parsonages.

Somehow, womanhood really "took" with me. It wasn't only that I grew up in a time when women's roles were more closely related to the home than they are today. I wasn't just emulating the apron-clad TV mom of the '50s. As a little girl, I spent hours dressing dolls and serving tea parties. During my teen years, I loved learning to bake and cook.

To this day, I believe it is a God-given desire in a woman to fashion a home and to lovingly fill it with warmth and beauty for all who enter..

Understandably, my hopes for our life in the little red house were high.

## Out of Reach

That certain "something" I'd felt inside me just after we moved increased as I began to notice a growing aloofness in Howard. As a newly appointed vice president of marketing and sales for a west coast tour company, he was naturally feeling the pressure as a young executive on the rise in the burgeoning travel industry.

After work, when he pulled into the driveway, I'd rush to the door to let him in, eager to hear about his day and share mine with him. When I'd ask him how his day went, he'd give me a perfunctory "Okay," or "Just great," then brush my face with a quick peck on the cheek and walk past me into the bedroom or kitchen.

I couldn't figure out why this talkative, breezy guy, the one with whom conversation was always so easy in our dating days, was suddenly not talking.

This was the man who used to entertain me with his nonstop stories and jokes. This was the man who, during our courtship, would twirl me around and plant a big kiss on my cheek and beam me a dazzling smile. Now, within a few brief months, he had become more than untypically quiet. He had become emotionally unavailable.

More than once I pursued him with words, on into dinner, just trying to connect. I tried to find the Howie I knew, the upbeat, happy-go-lucky guy I married. But all my conversational gambits dropped at my feet like unopened parachutes.

As the weeks wore on, I began to feel a quiet desperation for that missing closeness. Like someone lost in a desert of need, I looked to Howard as my well, certain he held the elusive water that would satisfy my thirst for affirmation and affection. If only I could bring up the bucket.... But I couldn't even turn the crank.

I couldn't have known then what even Howard didn't recognize—that he was hurting from the unnamed pain in his childhood. Now, with his responsibilities as a husband, father and sole provider of a growing household, he suffered silently from anxiety and a sense of growing inadequacy.

But I didn't see that. I couldn't see that. So I tried harder.

## Alone Together

In one sense, our little red house was my beginning place. At last I could indulge my domestic creativity. At last I could create a home.

I spent my days baking Howard's favorite things. I sewed for our baby, who was due to arrive in less than three months, and worked in our garden. One thing I never doubted about myself was my competency to create a warm domestic atmosphere.

However, I began to feel increasingly incompetent in the area of our personal relationship. Somehow, in spite of all my efforts, the one thing I really wanted eluded me: intimacy. A warm, loving connection with my husband.

One night, shortly after we moved in, I edged over to Howard's side of the bed and extended my arm to massage his back. "Howie, we're going to be happy in this house, aren't we?" I moved my hand up to stroke his shoulder and neck with my fingertips.

Howard stiffened. He pulled his arms snugly to his side and mumbled, "We could have knocked down the price, but basically we did okay."

I leaned over and planted a little kiss on his back. "Thanks, Howie, this home means a lot to me."

But there was no response from my husband except a quiet, "Hey, I'm tired...okay?" His words weren't harsh, but they puzzled me. I couldn't understand this new distancing. It was as if a heavy curtain had dropped between us. Howard was on one side and I was on the other, feeling abandoned.

It was spring and we'd been in the red house five months, but instead of growing closer together, we were drifting apart. Negative thoughts gnawed at my mind. Was it me? Had I done something wrong? One question I barely dared ask myself: Am I terribly ugly as a pregnant woman?

Most of the time, I felt too humiliated to bring up the subject of "us" again. But once, when I mustered the courage to ask Howard one more time why he was aloof, he looked at me blankly for several seconds. Then he said quietly, "Jane...I don't know."

## A Moment of Joy

Our relationship may have mystified me, but I was sure about one thing with Howard: He really loved children. His reaction at seeing his new baby daughter was wonderfully spontaneous.

In the early morning hours of May 18, 1960, our baby, Lisa, arrived and, for the first two days, Howard wore a nonstop, full-faced grin. My spirits lifted with his. "Jane, she is so cute," he said repeatedly.

Fathers didn't have the easy hospital access to newborns in those pre-bonding days that they have now. Even so, Howard's delight was obvious. Every day he walked with me down to the nursery, pressed his face against the window, fixed his gaze on our little daughter, and shook his head in wonderment.

"Look at her sleeping like an angel." He'd pause to cast his eye on the current crop of newborns snug in their cribs. "She's really the prettiest one here." He may have been slightly prejudiced.

## Beginning Again

We drove home with baby Lisa in my arms and Jeff in the back seat. Would this miracle of childbirth mean a new start for Howard and me? My face flushed with anticipation as we rounded the corner of our street and caught sight of our little red house.

Home. How I loved all I wanted it to mean. Maybe we would be set now. Two children, Howard's job going well, a comfortable place to live. I made up my mind to be positive. *It's going to go well for us*, I thought. *I just know it.*

That hope propelled me with new energy to cope with the late-night feedings and all the extra work involved with a new baby. I even pushed myself to exercise so I'd get back into shape, convinced that real change was—if not immediate—just around the corner for Howard and me. I would make it happen.

As Howard's job responsibilities increased, his travel schedule kept pace. Sometimes he'd be gone for a few days. At other times, he'd be gone for more than a week. Meanwhile, with one young child and a new baby to handle, I really missed him.

Lisa was barely two months old when he left on a three-week trip to Alaska.

One day, shortly before he was due back, I found myself going under with the same old feelings of abandonment, until an idea hit me. Why not surprise Howard with a special "welcome home" dinner and evening with just the two of us? It had been eons since we'd taken time to really sit and talk.

The day before Howard was due back in town, preparing his favorite foods took priority. I was convinced this was going to be the evening when I would turn things around in our relationship, when that wonderful spark between us would return.

Mercifully, the day Howard was expected home, Jeff and Lisa went down for their naps without a whimper. I had plenty of time to peel apples for a pie and get the pot roast on. Just before dinner, I bathed and dressed the kids and left them playing quietly in the bedroom while I fixed my hair.

Howard's car pulled into the driveway. There he was, my husband, the man I loved, looking road-tired as he wearily carried his bags into the living room. He gave me a quick kiss before Jeff pounced on him with a whoop. "Daddy!"

As Howard took a shower and unpacked in the bedroom, I managed somehow to get Jeff into bed with a promise that "Daddy will play with you tomorrow night."

I had just put the plates on the table and lit the candles when Howard came into the kitchen wearing slacks and a sport shirt. Out of the corner of my eye, I looked for a smile, a wink or some kind of expressive recognition. I was looking for some indication of an emotional connection.

As we sat down, his eyes avoided mine. Instead, they passed over the pot roast in front of him and slid over to the homemade apple pie on the counter. Then, after his first bite, the compliments flowed. But they weren't about me, not even about us. "Wow, Jane, restaurant food will never compare to your cooking."

Just before dinner, I had been ravenous, but that night I toyed with my food as we talked about his trip, the flight, the yard and finally the weather. *This is just like it's always been,* I thought. I could feel disappointment rising within me as tangible as mercury in a thermometer.

Howard finished his pie, pushed his chair back from the table and headed out to the front yard. My heart sank to the floor as I sat with my eyes riveted to the skirt of my dress. I swallowed hard and felt a lump form in my throat.

I wanted to scream, "Don't you even see me?!" But I didn't. I just listened to the flap of the screen door as it shut behind him.

I sat motionless at the table for a few minutes. When I finally stood up, I sensed life draining out of me. My head whirled.

I looked at the water goblets in my hand as I carried them numbly to the sink. *I'm as empty as you are,* I thought as I slipped them in the dish pan.

# *Dark Waters*

In the weeks that followed, I felt like I was swimming the English Channel in mid-December. I wondered if I'd reach shore before dying of hypothermia.

Shore. Where was shore?

Even then, I was still certain I knew. It was a home where a husband looked up over his evening newspaper and, in a voice exuding caring, said, "Jane, do you know how much I love you?" It was a place where my deepest needs would be filled to overflowing with unconditional love, where my inner emptiness would dissipate under the tender care of my husband.

I thought I'd be safe forever inside that little red house with Jeff, our new baby, Lisa and, most of all, Howard.

But I was wrong.

Ironically, it was here, where I expected to be the happiest, that I encountered the strongest, most gnawing pain of my young life. Somehow I had to find a way out of the darkness.

# $\mathscr{T}$HE $\mathscr{F}$AMILY $\mathscr{T}$REE

Emotional scars and the accompanying pain don't just material-
ize out of vapor; they come from somewhere. Like rings in the
cross section of a giant redwood tree, they are telling records of
the traumas and storms in our lives.

David Seamands, in his book, *Healing of Damaged Emotions*,
points us to this example from nature:

> In most of the parks the naturalists can show you a cross
> section of a great tree they have cut, and point out that the
> rings of the tree reveal the developmental history, year by
> year. Here's a ring that represents a year when there was a
> terrible drought. Here are a couple of rings from years
> when there was too much rain. Here's where the tree was
> struck by lightning. Here are some normal years of
> growth. This ring shows a forest fire that almost destroyed
> the tree. Here's another savage blight and disease. All this
> lies embedded in the heart of the tree representing the
> autobiography of its growth.[1]

"And that's the way it is with us," continues Seamands. "Just a few minutes beneath the protective bark, the concealing, protective mask, are the recorded rings of our lives."

## *The Perfect Family*

No one is born into a perfect family. In the human realm, we are all deprived of the kind of unconditional love we crave—the kind that only God provides. Sin has left its poisonous bite, its insidious scars on every generation. Parents don't love perfectly, and children don't always perceive their love clearly.

When parents do not, or cannot, spend time developing loving relationships, or where there is turmoil in the home, the simple truth is the children are affected.

Almost without exception, they will grow up feeling emotional pain in place of the security and love they need. In a word, they will feel deprived.

Have you ever felt that way as an adult? As if you're not worth the attention or love of others? As if they really shouldn't take the time to bother with you?

I remember a special birthday. Some friends of ours took Howard and me out to dinner. When we got home, I took one innocent step forward into our darkened family room and suddenly the lights flicked on and a group of friends chorused, "Surprise!"

As I gazed around at a roomful of delighted faces, I felt an instant crosscurrent of emotions: Joy and gratitude for their loving affirmation of me, yes, but I confess I also felt a twinge of embarrassment. Their love and friendship was the very thing I didn't deserve. Yet, it was exactly what I needed.

These feelings of not being worth anyone's time or effort haunted me most of my life. I can't pinpoint the moment they crept in, but I know they appeared at an early age—and that I learned early to cover them.

## My Story

That's my story. Like the redwood tree that hides its history inside its healthy-looking bark and branches, the outside indicators of my childhood were all tidily in place: two capable parents, food to eat, a house to live in and clothes to wear.

I may have looked like a quiet little girl bouncing through life with plaid ribbons tied at the end of my pigtails, but the real me, the one unknown to anyone but God, was aching inside. Never mind the ribbons in my hair; I had a larger ribbon knotted around my heart. It read: "Hurting Child."

Poor innocent child. Who's responsible? Who's to blame?

Isn't that the question our litigious society would ask? It's the same question the disciples asked Jesus about the man born blind: "Who sinned, this man or his parents, that he should be born blind?" (John 9:2, *NASB*). Where can we point the accusing finger?

## Blaming or Healing?

Someone wisely said, "While you blame, your wounds can't heal."

Clearly, my parents—and Howard's—made mistakes. Clearly, every other parent in the world has made and will make mistakes, myself included.

Blaming parents, however, is not on my agenda. Looking at reality is.

Our impressionable growing-up years can hold invaluable clues to understanding the people we are today. If there have been hurts, as there were in my life—and surely most everyone else's—the truth is that these cannot be healed if they are denied, or if those who hurt us are not forgiven.

## The Healing, Backward Look

An honest look backward at the family I grew up in has helped me identify some of the hidden rings of my life.

Meet my father, Tom Williamson. If you saw his picture in the family photo album, you'd be drawn to this handsome young man from Belfast, Ireland, with dark wavy hair and snapping blue eyes. If by some technological marvel, you could hear him talk or sing, you would be enchanted by his quick Irish wit and his soaring tenor voice.

Dad's real love was music. While it was a lofty goal for those times, he wanted, more than anything, to be an opera singer. He studied music in school. His family saw his potential and encouraged him, but voice and music lessons had to be paid for and there was no money left over from a budget already stretched to support a family of six. Dad had no choice; he had to earn a living. So as many young men in Belfast did at that time, he went to work in the Harland and Wolff Shipyards, along with his father, who had helped to build the Titanic.

## A Life-Changing Meeting

Then, in the early 1920s, something happened that forever changed Tom Williamson's life. Revival swept through Northern Ireland.

W.P. Nicholson, a well-known evangelist of the time, preached powerful messages each night in the Newington Presbyterian Church. Word spread fast and the hungry crowds packed the pews. Shipyard workers came in droves, directly from work, in order to find a seat. They came carrying newspapers to fold around themselves so their dirty work clothes wouldn't stain the pews.

Each night, when Reverend Nicholson gave the altar call, he did something unheard of in the staid Presbyterian church of that day. He asked those accepting Christ to stand and say, "Mr. Nicholson, I take Jesus Christ as my Savior."

On April 2, 1922, Dad could no longer stay in his seat. Wild horses couldn't have held him back. He leapt to his feet and professed that he would "take Jesus."

And Jesus "took" my father.

Dad was never the same. His heart was instantly captured by the Savior and inflamed with His love. What is more, he couldn't keep quiet about it. Dad must have told us his testimony a hundred times. And every time he told it, his eyes filled with tears when he repeated the unforgettable moment when, as he put it, "For the first time in my life, I heard the gospel."

Shortly after his conversion, Dad left Ireland with his father to look into the possibility of living in the United States. The family was to follow. But when Dad's mother became ill, his father returned to Belfast. Tom stayed on and settled in Flint, Michigan.

Dad was a modest man, not given to seeking the adulation of others, yet he was unembarrassed about his reputation as "the fiery Irish evangelist." We were told and retold stories of how he stopped on the way home from work to preach on the street corners of Flint. These stories are still rich memories for me.

When Dad was unable to dismiss the Lord's call to ministry, he made a hard decision. He chose to lay aside his cherished dream of a musical career and became an ordained pastor in the Christian and Missionary Alliance denomination. His beginning pastorate was in Mount Vernon, a small town near Columbus, Ohio.

That first Sunday from his pulpit, Dad couldn't help but notice the talented church pianist, Mystel Burson. He thought her playing was extraordinary, and she was beautiful as well, with a mane of reddish-gold hair and a modest manner.

Her early pictures show her as a sparkling, fresh-faced young woman. When she and Dad met, Mystel was preparing to enroll in the prestigious Eastman School of Music in Rochester, New York. She wanted to pursue a lifelong goal to be a concert pianist.

# *Opposites Attract*

Their romance didn't exactly blossom overnight, but almost. These two musically gifted, bright young people who loved God, couldn't help but be attracted to each other. Tom, the fun-loving, witty Irishman, and Mystel, beautiful and talented though prone to worry, married and settled down in Mount Vernon, Ohio.

Early in their marriage, it became apparent that Tom and Mystel had two very different temperaments: An optimist had married a pessimist.

Dad, a man of passion, immersed himself in whatever he was doing. An unquenchable fire seemed to burn within him. He loved life and being around people, singing, and telling his zany jokes.

Mother took life seriously. She could be pleasantly social whenever the occasion demanded it, but she was never naturally gregarious like Dad. She simply could not comprehend her husband's easygoing Irish personality, his lightheartedness and his penchant for telling what she considered "corny" stories.

On top of that, her parents frequently bemoaned the fact that their talented daughter forsook a promising musical career to marry a "poor preacher." Mother struggled often with her insecurities and anxiety.

When my brother, Jimmy, was born, he won my parents' hearts immediately. Four years later, it was my turn.

Six weeks after I was born, Dad took a position as head of the music department at the Bible Training Institute in Nyack, New York. We lived there for two years, then moved to Akron, Ohio, where he became pastor of another Christian and Missionary Alliance Church.

The Akron photos depict us as one happy pastor's family, smiling and seeming to thrive in the activities of a demanding ministry. My blond, sensitive older brother, Jimmy, and I appear in pictures as scrubbed and dressed with care. "When you came," my mother used to tell me, "we knew then we had the perfect family—a boy and a girl."

Perfect?

My memories of myself during this period are meager. I felt alone much of the time, lost in the busyness swirling around me, isolated from the hub of all my parents' ministry activities.

Dad was well thought of in the denomination in Akron and gained further recognition as a music director as well as preacher, who led traveling choirs and quartets and gave public concerts.

Mother, insecure as always, but ever his faithful accompanist, trooped right along with him.

JUST LIKE THE RINGS OF A TREE THAT
SHOW BLIGHTED YEARS COVERED
BY THE BARK, UNDERNEATH OUR
SCRUBBED FAMILY FACADE MY FAMILY
WAS SHOWING SIGNS OF CRACKING.

Every morning Mother gave me some special time with her before she started her chores and other activities. I would sit high on a kitchen stool, while she brushed and braided my hair. We talked about my friends and I could tell her what was happening in school.

Family vacations were nonexistent. Even summers gave no respite. Instead of taking days off to camp or picnic like other families, we crisscrossed the country in the car so Dad and Mother could preach and sing at all the summer conferences.

There was no time for Jimmy and me to do the things kids do on hot, lazy days. We couldn't run down a path in the park with our arms flying from our sides. We couldn't squeal at the top of our lungs as we were pushed in a swing. There was no time to twirl around in the backyard and drop like dead men at our parents' feet.

What I remember most was sitting. We sat in the car, we sat in the pew, we sat in the social hall after the meetings.

## The Frozen Image

Cameras only capture an image frozen in time. They can't reproduce truth on film. I discovered later that there was much more to the picture than the handsome pastoral couple with the well-behaved children. Just like the tree ring that shows blighted years covered by the bark, underneath our scrubbed family facade the Williamson family was showing signs of cracking. Not having enough time to spend together as a family was taking its toll. Especially on me.

## A Hug on the Run

"Daddy, could you help me with my homework?"

I didn't scream or yell for his attention, but when I needed Dad, I'd try snagging him right after dinner, before he flew out the door to church.

"Let's see your arithmetic book, honey." For a few idyllic moments, I would squeeze up to Dad's side, tablet and pencil in hand, eager to hand him my book and paper, but even more desirous of having his attention.

"Oops, you can't subtract 6 from 74 without borrowing." He'd wink at me and shake his head. "Jane, you're my little apple blossom, do you know that?"

I loved those tender moments when he called me "Apple Blossom," but they were never long enough. He was the apple of my eye, my knight in shining armor. I adored him.

When Dad glanced at his watch and got up from the chair, I felt guilty for always wanting to prolong our time together. It was what I wanted more than anything else, to feel close to my daddy for just a little bit longer. *Couldn't I have more than a hug on the run?* I asked myself.

Many times I remember Dad putting down *my* books and gathering up *his.* "Sorry, honey, I can't take any more time now. I love you." He'd grab me for a quick squeeze and dash off.

A kind of subdued longing engulfed me as I watched my dad and mother disappear out the door, calling out their instructions to the baby-sitter as they rushed down the front steps to Bible study, choir practice or prayer meeting.

I wanted to talk with someone who had time to listen. I wanted more than a hug you grabbed for like a loaf of bread as you dashed in and out of a convenience store. Yet I sensed that my parents' lives were filled with important things to do, things much more important than I. It wasn't until later that I came to see why.

How could I tell anyone how I felt then? This was the man I idolized. My dad preached sermons that kept people on the edge of their seats. Everyone loved Tom Williamson.

Mother's gifted homemaking did not keep her from being nervous about the parsonage being "open for inspection," with people stopping by unannounced with hand-me-down clothes or vegetables from their gardens. During those visits, Mother's directions to Jimmy and me were explicit: "Mind your manners. Remember, you must set a good example."

Somehow we got the unspoken message that God Himself had ordered us to behave; we had to reflect His good name. After all, we were the pastor's children.

When Dad was home, he frequently secluded himself in his study to read, prepare sermons or write music. My ten-year-old head accepted it, but more than once I crawled into bed with a sad heart and a mind full of questions without answers. *Does Daddy really love me? Doesn't he want to spend time with me?*

Then I'd make myself picture Dad up in the pulpit, the place I saw him the most, preaching about the mysteries of God's love in eloquent language. Then I'd fall asleep with his shining face etched in my mind. It wasn't the same as cuddling up on his lap, but it was the best I had.

## Good-Bye Akron, Hello Glendale

The church in Akron grew numerically and spiritually under Dad's ministry, and both Mother and Dad forged many strong friendships in the community.

However, a large church in southern California asked Dad to come, and, finally, he decided that the Lord was speaking to him, directing him to "go West."

How we hated to leave Akron! As an 11-year-old who came to Akron at age 2, it was the only home I remembered. My brother, Jimmy, and I were comfortably settled in school, doing well with our studies. I'd made a few close friends, and Jimmy had a thriving circle of teenage companions.

For pastors' families, moving goes with the territory, and our family could not escape this ritual. When it came time to say good-bye to Akron, a large crowd turned out for a farewell reception for us. Dad, Mom, Jimmy and I stood side by side as every person filed past to give us their tearful good-byes.

## Tough Going

We arrived in Glendale only to discover this would be a difficult season in our lives.

Many of the promises made to my dad went unfulfilled. Nothing seemed to work out the way we expected. The first year was particularly painful. We couldn't seem to make friends like we did in Ohio, and we were homesick for those we'd left behind. Many lonely evenings, the four of us walked the streets in silence, holding hands and wondering if our hearts would ever mend.

Of all of us, Jimmy was hit hardest. At 15, he struggled to make his way into established peer groups, but he couldn't penetrate them, either at school or with the young people at church.

Somehow this fresh-scrubbed, sensitive boy from the Midwest just didn't fit in. Jimmy's inability to make the transition caused him to look elsewhere for acceptance. Unfortunately, kids whose influence was anything but positive accepted him, and soon drinking, smoking and staying out late became his way of life.

Jimmy's behavior added pain to an already stressful time in our family. The move from Akron to California was now weighted with a new crisis point.

My parents were struggling. Dad was involved in activities from morning to night. In order to keep up with Dad, Mother stepped up her pace. She added to her crowded days by entertaining parishioners often. She fed and housed visiting pastors and missionaries. Always aware that someone from church could pop in at anytime, she drove herself to keep the house immaculate.

More and more, my parents' innate differences in temperament emerged as friction points in their marriage. The result was an uneasy tension that would build until one snapped at the other, only to be met with hurt looks or quiet withdrawal.

## A New Danger

Stress, by its nature, doesn't idle in neutral. Not only was our home fueled by it, it was accelerating.

During this vulnerable period in my parents' relationship, a woman in the congregation began to make deliberate, flattering overtures toward Dad.

In today's world, this incident would be labeled an unwise friendship or perhaps a mild flirtation. It certainly was not, in any sense of the word, an affair. But this woman, in her witty—and deliberate—manner, briefly turned Dad's head by affirming his preaching and musical talents in a flattering way.

Mother gradually grew aware of what was taking place. She already felt insecure about Dad's love for her, and this woman's actions served to underscore her doubts and weaken their marriage relationship even further.

A full-blown marital crisis erupted under our roof.

Instead of snapping followed by silence, tears and angry accusations ricocheted through our house. The worst part was that I was in the middle, caught in the crossfire of two hurting people that I loved.

## Caught in the Crossfire

"Do you think Dad loves me?" Mother turned to me, a pre-teenager, for her emotional solace. Then, in a voice filled with hurt, she would say, "Nobody really cares about me."

Dad, in his own way, also turned to me as he made asides about Mother's nervousness and constant fretting.

If it wasn't their own relationship they talked about to me, it was Jimmy and their anguish over his behavior. Jimmy, in turn, frustrated with parents who he felt didn't have time for him, confided in me, too. "All they want," he said, "is for me to march to their own little drumbeat."

Typical of most families in the midst of relational dysfunction, all three family members elected a go-between. And it was me.

As a 12-year-old girl, I hated this emotional battleground. I was caught in the middle, waving a small white handkerchief of truce in every direction, but nobody seemed to notice.

## A Pocket of Grace

Looking back now, I see a pocket of grace in the midst of that whirlwind, a tender touch of the Lord to a little girl longing for her parents' love, yet caught between two hurting adults.

My Aunt Ina and Uncle Bill and their daughter, June, the cheeriest Irish folk in the world, came to stay with us while their new home was being built. In the midst of the pervading gloom and doom in our household, they greeted me each morning with an uplifting word, a hug, or sometimes a lilting Irish folk song. It was as if someone had thrown open the door to let in the sunshine with a fresh spring breeze.

I got real hugs from Aunt Ina and Uncle Bill. During those few short months they were with us, their stability and accepting love touched me in a deeply meaningful way.

## A Time of Repentance

Every storm has its fallout. Downed branches. Power outages. Overflowing gullies. Eventually something tangible had to give in our home, too. Mother was on the verge of a nervous breakdown, the culmination of nearly two years of harboring undealt-with issues in her life. Dad realized her fragile condition and came to his senses. He finally saw his foolish behavior for what it was: selfish, destructive, sinful.

Broken and deeply repentant, Dad resigned from the Glendale church and served as a traveling speaker within the denomination, while Mother, Jimmy and I returned to Ohio for several months.

## The Unseen Fallout

And me? I didn't realize the toll these years had taken on me at the time. I do remember one day shortly before my thirteenth birthday, standing in front of the hall mirror and studying myself. There I was in hand-me-down clothes, with my childhood braids gone and, in their place, a frizzy perm. I looked straight at the reflected Jane and thought, *Who are you, little girl?* You have borrowed clothes, a borrowed house and borrowed parents. No wonder no one hugs you.

Most psychologists know now that even very young children are incredibly perceptive about picking up signs of stress in their parents' marriage. All I know is I felt absolutely trapped, pulled to be loyal to both parents and to a brother I dearly loved.

On one hand, I wanted to set everything right; on the other hand, I wanted desperately for all the hurt and anger to go away forever. I felt responsible, as if I were the only stable one in the storm. What I wanted was a family, but I couldn't fix all their problems.

One day, alone on my bed, I made a quiet decision, not realizing at that young age that it was actually a vow. The results of that vow affected me emotionally for years.

I swore to myself that no man would ever hurt me the way Dad hurt my mother.

# $\mathcal{M}$AKING $\mathcal{C}$HOICES

The crisis in southern California was over. The storm that rocked our home for nearly two years passed, sweeping away with it the debris of pain and misunderstanding. The winds of adversity, which had battered Mother and Dad's marriage so strongly, subsided.

In the calm that followed, a new love and commitment began to take root within the rich soil of understanding and acceptance.

Back in the Midwest, it was a new era and a time for healing for our family. Jimmy, now 19, lived with us only briefly in Ohio before he joined the Air Force and headed for Korea.

Dad's growing reputation as a preacher of the Word made him a sought-after speaker. One admiring colleague told him, "When I hear you preach, Tom, my preaching sounds like the squeaking of a gate."

Word of Dad's preaching quickly spread to the West Coast. We'd been in Ohio only a year when he accepted a call to a church in Berkeley, California. Once more, Mother packed and labeled our furniture and household goods. Once more, the big van pulled up to our house and loaded us up for another cross-country move.

# A New Mission

Dad's call was to a new mission church which did not yet have a parsonage. Because of this, Mother, Dad and I moved in with a family in the congregation for three months, until church housing became available.

Their home was lovely and the family, gracious to us. Carla, their daughter, who was three years older than I, shared her room with me. Besides offering her friendship, she introduced me to a whole new world—a world of cashmere sweaters, wool pleated skirts, Spaulding white buck shoes—all the "in" clothes for Berkeley High School girls in the '50s. It was heady stuff for me, and it wasn't long before all my old feelings of personal deficiency resurfaced, rushing out of hibernation to parade before me. Again, in my mind, I was the little girl standing before the hall mirror, dressed in hand-me-downs with that old feeling of not being "enough."

# A New Chance in College

After graduation from Berkeley High School, I enrolled in what was then Seattle Pacific College, a small Christian liberal arts school nestled alongside the Lake Union Ship Canal. It was my first introduction to Seattle, a beautiful setting, and for me, a socially freeing environment.

For the first time in my life, I was comfortable with my contemporaries, young people reared with the same values I was. In high school, because of all the things I couldn't do as Pastor Williamson's daughter, I'd always felt like an outsider. In Seattle, in a Christian college, I felt I could freely enter into all the school activities. I blossomed in this environment, and soon I was participating in many aspects of campus social life as well as sports.

My freshman year flew by. However, by June I was uncertain of my academic direction and concerned about the financial burden my schooling placed on my parents and another family who shared the costs. I decided to return to California and look for a job.

I found a position in downtown Oakland as a secretary in an office. I was now a young working woman, continuing to live with my parents, but bringing home a regular paycheck.

Without warning, I was then thrown into a situation that raised terror in my heart.

## A Word from God?

One morning, while Dad was having his usual coffee at the local bakery, a young man joined him at his table and the conversation soon turned to their faith. After that, the two men met often to discuss spiritual matters. Sometimes they'd go for a walk together; sometimes Dad invited him home.

When I met this young man, I felt oddly uncomfortable around him—as did my mother. He seemed to take the words and counsel of my father to a mystical realm that lacked reality and balance. I was put off by this and by the way he seemed absorbed with his own spirituality.

One day, out of the blue, I received a letter from him—a letter insisting that God told him I was to be his wife.

I was stunned. I couldn't believe what I was reading. I hadn't the slightest romantic interest in this young man. Yet, I was shaken by his insistence that God was issuing this edict. At that point in my life, I had a faulty perception of God and His will. I believed He arbitrarily made decisions for a person's life, that He took no personal interest in us.

You can understand why I was so frightened. Here I was, an 18-year-old girl with my whole life ahead of me. Then someone tells me I'm to be married because it's God's will. Sheer terror gripped me.

That evening, I went to Dad for counsel, fully trusting him to come to my rescue. "Dad, this is really scary. What should I do?" I remember looking into Dad's eyes, confident that he would immediately label this man's idea as preposterous—and certainly not God's will.

Incredibly, Dad hesitated. A cold chill ran through me. Was he not going to come to my rescue?

The silence continued.

My father, a strong man of God, couldn't risk intervening in case he might somehow miss God's leading. He simply stepped back and let the pronouncement stand as if it *were* the will of God.

I panicked. Here was the man I so admired and looked up to, the one who represented God to me, the one I counted on for spiritual wisdom. He gave me no counsel, no advice, just silence.

I interpreted his silence to mean one thing: God Himself had acquiesced to this pronouncement. I was being signed over as a pawn in what felt like an arranged marriage. After all, who could argue with God?

A suffocating panic seized me, and as the months passed, my panic grew. It was as if I were marching toward a cliff I knew was there. Others, too, knew of the danger, but no one yelled a warning. I was walking toward the brink alone in a thick silence.

## *The Not-So-Great Escape*

Then, one day, a new young man started attending our church. Everyone, including me, seemed drawn to his twinkling brown eyes and ready smile.

I now realize I was drawn to him largely out of my own panic, like one teetering on the edge of a dangerous precipice is drawn to a lifeline thrown in her direction. But within a few short months of our meeting, the young man with the ready smile and I were married.

As you can well imagine, we were two young people ill-prepared to enter marriage. It was a brief but disastrous experience. Two years and a child later, we separated, then divorced.

Here I was, a pastor's daughter, raised in an evangelical Christian home. I'd spent most of my life trying to please my parents and now, after one wrong choice—a choice made out of panic and fear—a feeling of absolute failure and guilt engulfed me.

This was a turn I thought my life would never take. I felt permanently marked.

Swamped by a thunderous onslaught of guilt and shame, it would take years and the cleansing blood of Jesus to heal me.

## Starting Again

I was single again.

I was a woman with no rings gleaming on her finger, yet one bright ray of sunshine glowed in my dark world—my blond, blue-eyed Jeff. Four months old, he was the light of my life.

Where was God in all my confusion? I know now what I didn't know then: He was close at hand. The Lord was right there, weeping over my sin and pain, yearning to draw me to Himself. He was reaching out to me, His arms open and His hands extending unconditional love and forgiveness. My perception then, however, was that God was disinterested in the hurts and wounds of people.

I related to God at that time much as I did to my earthly father: He had time for everyone else, but not for me. As far as I was concerned, I was on my own.

## Facing Reality

There were some very practical issues I would have to handle on my own. Overnight, it seemed, I had become a single mother who needed an apartment, a job and someone to care for her baby while she worked. A tall order, but I was determined to make my own way and not be a burden to my parents. After all, I reasoned, I'd already let them down enough.

Fortunately, jobs were plentiful then and I was able to find what I needed: loving care for Jeff, a small apartment and a position with a travel agency close by. Life went on. I was busy and finances were tight, but I was making it—barely.

I'd been at the travel agency a month or so when I started having coffee and an occasional lunch with Genevieve, a gracious young Australian woman. As a busy single mother with little time for a social life, I relished opportunities for stimulating adult conversation. Genevieve and her husband were avid travelers. They'd work for awhile in one place, then move on to see more of the world.

Although I'd crisscrossed the U.S. with Mother and Dad, I'd never traveled overseas, so listening to Genevieve's stories was much like watching a fascinating special on "National Geographic," narrated with a delightful Australian accent.

One morning, in an offhanded way, Genevieve mentioned her boss, Howard Hansen, who'd been spending a lot of time out of town on business. "I'm eager to have you meet him, Jane. He's so easy to get to know, you'd really enjoy him."

While I appreciated Genevieve's intent, meeting men wasn't on my agenda. As far as I was concerned, I'd be single the rest of my life. So mindful was I of my marriage failure that, if any man had seriously approached me at that time, I would have run in the other direction—fast.

As the months passed, however, others in the agency dropped comments about Howard, and Genevieve remained quietly persistent. "Wait till you meet Howie, Jane. You're going to love him." By now, I was curious.

One day, Genevieve brought a tall, broad-shouldered, blue-eyed blond with a California suntan to my desk. "Jane, I want you to meet Howard Hansen." From our first meeting, we had a relaxed rapport. Soon we were chatting comfortably over the water cooler, then at coffee and occasionally over lunch.

At the office or at lunch, I couldn't help but notice how others also warmed to Howard. He seemed to be the life of the party, with time to joke or chat with everyone. This blond Dane with the sunny disposition and a warm, affectionate nature began to stir my heart in spite of myself.

Then one morning, Howard stopped by my desk and invited me to dinner.

As he and I began seeing each other, "dinner out" became a home-cooked meal at my apartment. For a mother of a little one who had to pay for a baby-sitter, going out anywhere was a real luxury. A meal at home, with Howard across from me at the table and Jeff between us in his high chair, was hardly a romantic evening, yet it seemed easy and natural.

Howard and I took turns helping Jeff cut his meat, then wiping off his sticky hands. During those moments in between, we squeezed in our own adult conversation.

Howard's gentle, caring manner, especially toward Jeff, comforted me in an indescribable way. Before dinner, the two of them would laugh and giggle on the floor, sometimes tossing a ball or playing peek-a-boo. They were like two bear cubs, Howard performing with a tender abandon, and Jeff playing with exuberant delight.

What a contrast with Dad, I thought. Dad, who was the center of attention outside the home, sought solitude to study or listen to symphonic music, as soon as he walked through the parsonage doors. At the time, I felt he was closing himself off from us.

Hearing Howard's laughter inside my little apartment gave me a real lift, while other signs of his caring for us melted my heart.

One winter evening, after we'd picked up Jeff from the baby-sitter's and walked into my apartment, Howard reached in ahead of me to switch on the lights. Nothing happened.

I knew immediately that it wasn't a burned out light bulb and was glad the darkness hid my embarrassment. After an awkward few seconds, I managed to mumble, "Howard, there's a problem: I've been waiting for my next paycheck before I mailed in the light bill."

Without a sign of reproach, Howard set my groceries on the kitchen counter, turned on his heel and was out the door, calling after me, "Be back in half an hour, Jane." And he was, carrying in his hand the receipt for the paid-up light bill.

Mix all Howard's qualities together and it's easy to see why I fell in love with this man who cared for me so generously and

HOWARD AND I BOTH BROUGHT EMOTIONAL BAGGAGE INTO OUR MARRIAGE. YEARS LATER, EVEN THE FACADE OF SOPHISTICATED SOFT-SIDED LUGGAGE COULDN'T DISGUISE THE SINFUL CONTENTS.

who so obviously cared for my son. Ten years older than I, Howard was settled in a good job with a promising future—and he was a faithful churchgoer.

We were married in February, 1959, and off for a brief honeymoon in Carmel, California.

## Bringing in the Baggage

Picture the honeymoon couple: Blissfully, they return home from their first few days together as husband and wife. He carries her over the threshold and gently sets her down in the entryway. They embrace and spend a long moment gazing into each other's eyes. Finally the bride whispers sweetly, "Darling, we need to bring in the suitcases."

The groom dashes to the car, and deposits the contents in the front hall, saying with pride, "I guess we're ready to start our married life. I just brought in the baggage."

Little does any honeymoon couple know at the time, that just as they carry their suitcases in the front door, they also bring in their emotional baggage—not into the house, but into the marriage. This baggage doesn't fill the car trunk, and it doesn't contain jazzy sport outfits, beautiful lingerie or glamorous evening wear. In fact, none of it is pretty to look at, especially once it's out of the bag and draped across its owner.

Howard and I both brought emotional baggage into our marriage. "Stuff" we'd been accumulating since childhood. Piece by piece, item by item, our first hurts and emotional pain went into a little cardboard suitcase. Through our teen years, in duffel bags, we continued to pack in more hurts, fears, pain, false perceptions of ourselves and others. Finally, we added layers of self-protective strategies. The bags filled up.

Elaborate coping mechanisms, masks to cover up, layers to hide flaws—they all went in. Years later, when we were long entrenched in behavior patterns and beliefs that directed our lives, even the facade of sophisticated soft-sided luggage couldn't disguise the sinful contents.

## Howard's Story

Howard, too, was reared in a pastor's family. The youngest of three boys, he grew up in the Midwest. If you were to open the Hansen photo album, you'd see Howard's dad, a first generation Danish immigrant. A man of personal strength, he knew what he believed and didn't mind telling others.

A sincere, born-again believer, Howard's father was, nevertheless, exacting with his boys. His parenting was not untypical of an era when a high premium was placed on hard work and being obedient. He was a strict disciplinarian; Howard remembers how his father spoke harshly when obedience was not forthcoming.

"If I didn't obey my father," Howard says, "I'd be spanked or disciplined in some other way. That was something I really feared. As a 'preacher's kid,' I knew I had to be good."

Howard's mother was the understanding nurturer. Howard grinned with delight when he recalled the way she warmly cared for him. "She was a quiet, gentle, very loving woman," he said. "That's probably why I hung around the kitchen so much. I liked being with her. I could always feel her love and sense her acceptance of me."

This woman always seemed to have time for Howard, whether it was reading to him, helping with his homework or talking with him in the warm glow of the kitchen.

To this day, his mother's words of unqualified praise echo in his memory. Once, as a 14-year-old, Howard took a washing machine motor and rigged it up to power his bike. He drove his new invention—something no one in town had seen—past her viewing spot on their Montana parsonage porch, and he glanced up for her response. He basked in her unfailing admiration: "Howard, you've done a wonderful job."

As much as his mother's praise meant to him, Howard secretly longed inside for some word of approval or acknowledgment from his dad.

"Like many men, my dad was unable to show much outward affection or give warm, affirming words to his sons," Howard says now. "He deeply cared for us and he would do anything for my mother, but affirmation from the head of the household, in an era of absolute obedience, was not considered a virtue." Still, Howard's sensitive boy's heart longed for open, honest conversation with his father.

Howard still remembers the familiar routine in the Hansen home. The day began with devotions at breakfast, with everyone, including Tippy the dog, in his appointed spot. Howard always wanted to eat quickly and leave the table because the whole process seemed so regimented. "We'd talk only about surface kinds of things, the weather, the church, sports. No one ever talked about how he felt, whether he was mad, sad or glad."

At school, Howard shrank when one of the kids would ask what his dad did for a living. When they did, he just mumbled, "minister," a word that told them that Howard couldn't go to the movies or join them in some of their activities. Since it was too awkward to just be one of the boys, he spent time with the men of the church, who took a lively interest in him and his projects.

The scene changed in later life. Whenever Howard visited his dad as an adult, he was immediately escorted downtown to be shown off to the barber, the grocer and the rest of his dad's friends having coffee at the bakery.

In his head, the adult Howard knew his dad was proud of him. Otherwise, he wouldn't be so eager to display his grown son. "But my emotional baggage was there to give me another message," Howard explains. "My heart still carried the stamp of the childhood perception that I wasn't important as a person, just as a performer."

Howard and I both learned to be performers, to play a role, in our childhoods. It was part of the baggage we brought with us into the little red house.

## A Physical Reaction

After Howard's homecoming from his Alaska trip, life for us continued in emotional isolation. More than once I recalled my valiant attempt to connect with him on his first night home with what I had hoped would be a special dinner. It was a painful memory.

I was soon, however, to experience another pain, a debilitating physical pain. It struck hard and I couldn't pass it off.

Howard, aware of my distress, mentioned it one morning as he was leaving the breakfast table. I could hear the worry in his voice. "Better check with the doctor, Jane. You've been doubled over with that pain for two weeks now." He was right. All my home remedies weren't touching my excruciating stomachache.

The doctor's words hit hard. "Mrs. Hansen, your test results are back. I'm sorry to tell you that your abdominal pain is caused by a bleeding ulcer." He paused to let the news sink in. "An ulcer is nothing to fool around with, and a bleeding ulcer...." The doctor reached for his prescription pad and sighed. "I know you have Lisa and Jeff to take care of, but somehow you're going to have to reduce the stress in your life. Why don't you and your husband get away from the kids for a weekend? A break will do you good."

It was my turn to sigh. In the '60s there wasn't yet the concern for the interrelatedness of physical and emotional well-being that there is in today's medical practices. Had there been, the doctor might have looked me square in the eye and said, "What's going on in your life?" But at that time, he assumed I was just another tired young mother.

"You need to fill this immediately." He placed the slip of paper in my outstretched hand. "I want you started on medication by this afternoon." Then, with a look at my resigned expression, he smiled gently. "Be encouraged, Mrs. Hansen, we see good results in a matter of a few weeks with this treatment and a bland diet."

As I put the kids in the car and drove to the drugstore, the doctor's words continued to ring in my ears: "You've got to reduce the stress in your life."

*Easy for you to say, Doctor. Have you ever had two little ones, a tight budget, a yard to keep up and a husband who seems as distant as the man in the moon?* My defensiveness surprised me, and I quickly rationalized that feeling. *After all,* I told myself, *this is a pretty big assignment for one woman.*

Back at home, I tucked Lisa and Jeff into bed. I lingered in their room, listening to the soft sounds of their breathing. I shut the door carefully, amazed at how quickly kids fall asleep. That day I was especially grateful; we all needed a break.

I wandered back into the living room, kicked off my shoes, and sank into the big overstuffed chair. Weary from the hectic morning, my body sagged with relief. But my mind stayed in motion. Like a dog with a bone, I wanted to keep chewing on this stress issue.

Quickly, I discarded the idea that running the house and taking care of children was that stressful. Homemaking satisfied me, even energized me. And the kids? Sure they were a handful at times, but wonderfully fulfilling, nevertheless.

Just then, a sharp pain jabbed me in the stomach with an

intensity I couldn't ignore. Neither could I ignore the moment of truth. Tears filled my eyes as I sat there on the sofa.

*My stomach may be hurting,* I thought, *but my heart is hurting more. I just can't let my marriage fail.* I knew all along that only one person could fix my excruciating heartache, and that was Howard.

## The Wounded Bird

I got up and wandered to the kitchen window. Outside in the thicket of the juniper hedge bordering our fence, a tiny sparrow seemed caught on something. I saw his little head snap back and forth in sharp, jerking turns. Curious, I opened the kitchen door, walked to the side of the house and inched quietly along the hedge.

What was wrong? Why did he stay put when he was in such obvious terror? Why didn't he fly from his prickly hideout?

Up close, I found my answer. His feathers, rumpled and mashed on his right side, parted just enough to expose his drooping wing hanging limply from his body. No wonder this little sparrow couldn't fly, he was wounded—too wounded to do the very thing he was created to do.

In many ways, I felt like that wounded bird, wedged into my own emotional hiding place. I felt restrained from entering into life fully, as I knew it was intended. Instead I repeatedly set myself up for a cycle of disappointment. I didn't see it then, but I worked hard to attract Howard's attention and, when I didn't get what I needed, I quietly retreated into myself. The place where I withdrew felt akin to a cold, damp cave. There, nothing could reach me.

Where was God? Surely the God who encouraged the little children to come to Him and who raised the little girl in Luke's Gospel from her deathbed, created me to soar. This same God who, I know now, had a plan for my life, also had infinite patience. Not put off by my flailing in the darkness, He could— and He did—wait until I came to the end of myself.

But I wasn't there yet.

## Only Temporary Silence

Busyness has a way of temporarily silencing pain. To take the edge off, I plunged into community and church activities.

Howard and I joined a Lutheran church in our neighborhood. Even though my father had pastored another denomination, I was willing to join Howard in the church tradition he'd known all his life.

Churches always need volunteers and there were plenty of slots where I could help out. I assisted at women's circle luncheons and receptions and was rewarded with good feelings of accomplishment, new friends to share with and, most importantly, a distraction.

## From Red to Yellow

We'd spent four years in our little red house. Jeff was going on eight, and it was time for him and four-year-old Lisa to have separate bedrooms. I was pregnant with our third baby when we sold "Little Red" and bought what we called "the yellow house on the hill." Here, two months after we moved in, our son Scott was born.

With a beautiful new baby and a new neighborhood, my spirits lifted. Karen and Jim, the couple next door, immediately reached out to us. Their home was filled with lovely paintings, interesting art pieces, as well as stimulating conversation. My world, so centered on home and family, expanded, thanks to these two.

Karen was ten years older than I and an accomplished artist. She shared her decorating savvy and fashion tips with me, stretching my horizons and helping me to grow in confidence as a woman. How I enjoyed that kind of nurturing friendship!

Howard continued to do well in the travel business. We lived in the yellow house only a few months before he received a promotion along with news of a transfer.

As regional sales manager for the tour company, he was assigned to a branch office in the Los Angeles area. Howard flew down to work in the L.A. area almost immediately. I was thrilled that he continued to be rewarded for his ability and hard work, but it meant another separation. The children and I were to wait in Seattle until the house was sold before we could join him.

## Back and Forth

During this time, Howard often flew home on weekends, ready for a break from the pressures of a new job. Invariably, I greeted him at the door, ravenous for adult conversation after spending all my time as a temporary single parent. But, as usual, I didn't know how to get him to open up.

"What's the new office like, Howie?"

He'd toss out a quick reply and head for the lawn mower. I knew by now that my hopes, high when he came home on Friday afternoon, would plummet to the ground by Sunday night.

I'd gotten to the place where I was hurting, too close to view my situation objectively. I blamed myself for the emotional poverty of my marriage and desperately searched for Howard's affirmation.

Howard pushed the lawn mower back and forth, back and forth across the lawn. How well I knew that familiar motion, only mine was done in my mind. I cut a wide swath in one direction for my personal insufficiencies. Then, turning in the opposite direction, I mowed my way back toward the side that affirmed me as a woman of value. One of these days, I thought, I'm going to mow myself down.

## A Seedling of Hope

Shortly before the last time he returned to California, Howard walked into our bedroom to pack his bag. With the house sold, the children and I were to join him as soon as the final papers were signed.

"Need anything from the laundry room?" I called.

"Nope. Got everything I need in the drawers here, Jane."

I stood in the bedroom doorway and stared at my husband,

memorizing his big build and blond hair and everything else I loved about him.

"I'm going to miss you, Howie."

The socks were on the bed in little rolls, and his face and hands were concentrated on gathering them together to put into his suitcase. He never looked up.

A few minutes later, Howard walked into the kitchen where I was peeling apples for the kids' snack. I could feel a burning in my stomach; my ulcer was acting up again.

"Time to leave for the airport," he said breezily. "I'm glad the kids are over their colds." He leaned against the counter next to me for a brief moment. "I'll be seeing you in a couple of weeks when you come to L.A."

He reached out to give me a quick hug.

I stiffened. Something strong and stony rose up inside me. A silent, inward groan phrased my pain: *Something's got to give.*

I took a deep breath, cleared my throat, and spoke quiet, decisive words: "Howard, I don't think I'll be coming to Los Angeles with you."

Howard's head bobbed forward with a start and he looked at me with a long, blank stare. His bright, blue eyes filled with tears. Like a man in slow motion, he walked toward the window where his hands, at a loss for a gesture, reached out nervously to finger the ledge.

I stood facing him, the half-peeled apple in my hand. The room was absolutely still as Howard looked out at the towering evergreens bending under the summer breeze. His halting voice finally broke the silence.

"I don't know what's wrong, Jane." He paused to swallow. "But things are going to get better in California. I promise you."

I glanced sideways at the rock garden just outside our Dutch door as the moments passed. Some wild violets caught my eye, poking up among the stones. They looked as fragile as I suddenly felt inside, but watching their brave little heads buck the wind prompted a seedling of hope in me.

# To California with a Promise

In the early 1960s, young people flocked to southern California with great expectations their lives would be different there.

I bet my entire future on that dream.

When Howard made me that promise in our kitchen in Seattle, I was at the end of my stamina; the pain in my heart, intense and unrelenting.

Howard left for California, and I began to arrange for our move from Seattle. A mix of hopes, dreams and fears accompanied me. *What if it didn't work this time?* I would have moved again with three young children, set up a home again, connected the wires of our daily lives to a new community, a new routine. *Could I do it?* Yes. *Could Howard and I work out our relationship?* That was still the gnawing, unanswered question.

The children and I flew into the Burbank Airport on a bright day in June 1964. By the time we'd been in Burbank two months, the warm, sunny days and relaxed, indoor-outdoor living soothed me into believing that I could give our marriage another try.

We moved into a spit-and-polish Cape Cod rambler on Tujunga Avenue. The street, shaded with trees, ran along the north edge of Burbank and was one of hundreds of little neighborhoods that stretched throughout the San Fernando Valley, just north of Los Angeles.

Living in southern California was a new existence for Howard and me. Life in a city bursting with possibilities in every direction was heady stuff for two pastors' kids. Suddenly, we found ourselves swimming in a pond bigger than either of us had ever seen.

## California Dreamin'

By 1965, thousands of young people had been lured to Los Angeles and San Francisco with a promise of a new future they could control. Already, the Beatles had appeared on "The Ed Sullivan Show" and changed music forever. The Beach Boys' hit, "Wish They All Could Be California Girls," was taken seriously by a new generation charmed by the beckoning arm of a city that promised eternal youth and endless horizons—a place where they could make their own rules.

During those years, British "mod" fashion became a trendy way to dress. Women wore pants called hip-huggers, crop tops, miniskirts and white go-go boots. Rock-and-rollers, hippies and surfers mixed it up together as parks and beaches came alive with spontaneous rock concerts. This was before the underside of drugs was known and, ignorant of the consequences, Los Angeles quickly became a nonstop party.

Howard's new position as manager of the southwest regional office meant that he commuted over the Hollywood Hills separating "the Valley" from Hollywood. His work opportunities kept him challenged while I was finding challenges of my own.

The balmy weather and casual lifestyle warmed the cocoon of

my being enough for me to experience a personal metamorphosis of sorts. At age 29, I was maturing and growing in confidence. Now I could jump in to be Lisa's Bluebird leader with ease or help with Jeff's Cub Scout troop. Our youngest, Scott, took swimming lessons and we spent many long, leisurely days at the beach. I felt deeply blessed with these three loving children.

Cooking became a new adventure. Jane, the young bride for whom tuna casserole and meatloaf were an accomplishment, became Jane the hostess who knew her chicken divan from beef bourguignonne. Comfortable with entertaining now, I looked forward to planning dinner parties for a growing circle of friends.

Even in Burbank, with many of its small-town ways still intact, the impact of Los Angeles brought Howard and me into a new social life with a variety of people— those in the entertainment industry, stock brokers, lawyers, plus an occasional colorful character thrown in, the kind southern California parties are known for.

Although our idea of play meant that we shared oceanside picnics and volleyball on Santa Monica Beach instead of love-ins and rock concerts, Howard and I were convinced that these people really knew how to have fun.

Even though we maintained many of the values we grew up with during our Burbank years, I was not yet open to the Lord's gentle guidance. I didn't know Christ personally then, so I pursued life on my terms in California, trying to make it fulfilling and meaningful.

I wanted to be happy, and under the warm sun and friendly chatter, I could almost fool myself that I was. But I'd been reared too long in a Christian home to be totally at peace about parts of our new lifestyle.

## A New Encounter

Howard and I joined a Lutheran church in Glendale, where I encountered an adventure of another kind. I was teaching Vacation Bible School that summer and was drawn into a circle of women who were undeniably filled with joy. This expression was so much different from the kind of surface emotion that passed for happiness among our friends. I needed to know why.

One day, on the way home in the car, I felt comfortable enough with one woman to ask her a simple question: "What's so different about you?"

Her response was direct. "Jane, I have received the baptism in the Holy Spirit."

My obvious interest invited her to continue talking about Jesus, and how His love filled her in a new and powerful way and

FOR THE FIRST TIME IN MY LIFE, I WAS
AWARE THAT GOD WAS REACHING OUT TO
ME IN A PERSONAL WAY.

how she had spoken in tongues, a gift the Holy Spirit had given her. I was intrigued, but wary. I had to admit there was nothing "flaky" about this woman, and I couldn't argue with the reality I saw in her. It was as if something had melted the bedrock of her being and fused into it a peace and joy I couldn't imagine existed.

As I pondered what I saw and what she said, I began to feel a quiet inner sense that surprised me with its normalcy; this experience was not only right, it was also for me.

But when? Or how? I had no idea.

## Back to the Future

We had lived in Burbank for almost four years when Howard walked in the front door with a surprise.

"Can you believe it?" he chortled. "We're moving back to Seattle."

It may have surprised me at first, but instinctively, I felt that something good lay ahead. Whether it was my association with these women or the sole working of the Holy Spirit, for the first time in my life, I was actually aware that God was reaching out to me in a personal way.

As our Burbank years had progressed, the never-a-dull-moment days, so exciting at first, became empty rituals of the chicly dressed telling glib jokes over afternoon cocktails. Like a slow leak in a car tire, the lack of substance in our lives in California deflated our early enthusiasm for the laid-back life. Despite our church ties, in those four years we knew little of a life that sustained us in an affirming, nourishing way.

God moved in my dissatisfaction. The night before the moving van came, my hands went to an old book of my dad's, *The Pursuit of God* by A.W. Tozer. The words on one yellowed page drew me like a parched plant to water:

We pursue God because, and only because, He has first put an urge within us that spurs us to the pursuit. "No man can come to me," said our Lord, "except the Father which hath sent Me draw him." And it is by this very prevenient drawing that God takes us from every vestige of credit for the act of coming. The impulse to pursue God originates with God, but the outworking of that impulse is our following hard after him.[1]

I closed the book and shut my eyes, but the words remained illuminated in my mind's eye: We pursue God because He draws us to Himself first. Was this really happening? Was God indeed drawing me to Himself?

I, who had not yet known a personal relationship with this God I'd heard of since childhood, fell to my knees beside our bed. Everything in my past and present narrowed to one anguished cry from my heart: "God, help me! Please help me to find You and know You personally as You really are."

I did not ask Him into my life that night, but I sensed then that I was finally on the right road in my journey. God was my only hope, and moving back to Seattle was an important step in His direction.

## Trudging On

Had I known that I would struggle through another year in Seattle, filled with emptiness and frustration, my heart might have failed right then. I still carried guilt around like rocks in a gunny sack. There were times when I wondered if my lack of peace, despite my efforts, was punishment for the failure of my first marriage.

Once we got settled in Seattle, I joined a small Bible study that met in women's homes. The group was congenial and the fellowship was warm, but our discussion centered on the intellect rather than the heart.

One morning, rather than keep my pain inside myself, I took a risk. I told the group what was going on in my life. I had no idea how much my hurt would show until my voice began to quaver and tears formed in my eyes.

An awkward silence followed. No one said a word. I dabbed a handkerchief to my eyes and took a deep breath.

In a few moments, as if nothing had happened, the discussion picked up right where it paused before I spoke.

After we adjourned, I walked to my car alone. I eased into the driver's seat and quickly drove away. My stiff outward composure, however, belied my inner turmoil. I was a woman in extreme pain. I hurt in my marriage and now, adding to my anguish, ten-year-old Jeff was developing problems, just as my brother Jimmy had done in Glendale years earlier.

As I drove along, the floodgates finally burst. Tears streamed down my face and watered my lap. I knew what I had to do: I had to get to God.

## The Healing Word

Back home, I immediately sat down at the kitchen table and poured myself a cup of coffee. I reached for my Bible and opened it aimlessly to the Book of Lamentations. My eyes fell directly on the third chapter, seventh verse: "He hath hedged me about, that I cannot get out; he hath made my chain heavy" (*KJV*).

Incredulous, I read it over several times. It was as if that Scripture had my name on it. That's exactly how I felt—wanting to run as far as I could, but totally trapped and hedged in.

There was no other word for what happened to me in the next few moments than "revelation." God spoke to me through His Word, transcending my mind and penetrating my heart. In a few brief minutes, Truth unraveled itself with unbelievable speed and undeniable clarity.

I glanced out the kitchen window at the backyard fence. All that had gone before me, the sin, the sorrow, the pain, the disappointment, was not what God wanted for me. But His love was using it to build fences, fences that hedged me into a relationship with Him. This was not a secondhand relationship interpreted through the minds and hearts of parents or friends, but a relationship for me alone!

I knew positively that I was about to experience God's love firsthand and feel His personal touch on my personal needs. I knew, too, that the key lay in knowing Jesus. Not the Jesus I knew about intellectually—the historical figure I'd met in Sunday School stories—but a Jesus I could know. Really know.

I poured myself another cup of coffee and opened to the New Testament. Here I was, a woman unfamiliar with her Bible, stumbling across life-giving passages at my kitchen table. I turned to Matthew and again read words directed at my heart. "Your heavenly Father knoweth that ye have need of all these things" (Matt. 6:32, *KJV*).

What a concept! It hit me with laser precision. And it kept expanding as I sat there reading. God was my Father. He had used an earthly mother and father to bring me forth, but I was really His. He was the Creator of everything, seen and unseen. He knew me like no one knew me. In His love, He allowed the circumstances of life to prod and shape this "good little girl" who always tried to do everything right, to a point of knowing she was a sinner in need of a Savior. Love was teaching me.

Like the father in the Prodigal Son story of Luke 15, my heavenly Father was waiting for me. I could relate to every line of that familiar parable. The son who squandered his inheritance in the far country finally came to his senses, saying "I will get out and go back to my father" (see v. 18). The story could have been written just for me.

But there's more. I began to feel the impact of the rest of this story: the extraordinary move on the father's part—that embarrassingly emotional move. Seeing his wayward son afar off, the father runs to him to embrace him (see Luke 15:20).

Loving Father, needy daughter. The Lord Himself and Jane. She was coming home to the Father and He had run out to meet her with His outstretched arms. He knew me inside out as no one else had—or ever would.

In that moment, sensing His presence with me in my kitchen, I knew He could instantly speak everything in my life into perfect order—every longing, every hurt, every frustration, every need I had. He did know me, that was true, and He could "fix" everything. But the passage in Matthew that so arrested my attention had more to say: I needed to seek first the kingdom of God and His righteousness and all these things would be added to me (see Matt. 6:33).

Joy Dawson, internationally known Bible teacher, has often said, "God loves desperate prayers." That morning, I closed my Bible and prayed one:

"Lord, if I never spend another happy day in this life, I am going to seek You and Your Kingdom first. And I choose to trust You to add to me what I need."

I had come home at last.

# A NEW DIMENSION

Remember that portion of John's Gospel—see 13:31–14:16—where Jesus tells His disciples He will be leaving them? News like that must have shaken these men! No doubt some were stunned to silence. Others, like Peter, Thomas and Philip, peppered their Master with questions: "Where are You going?" "Why?" And perhaps the most burning question in their hearts, "What's going to happen to us?"

Jesus' answer to His little ragtag band of followers isn't exactly overflowing with comfort:

> "They will put you out of the synagogue; in fact, a time is coming when anyone who kills you will think he is offering a service to God" (John 16:2).

Not only would Jesus be leaving them, He warned that the days ahead would be anything but a Sunday School picnic!

This wasn't your typical retirement party with gold watches and glorious predictions for the future; this was talk of separation, hardship and death. Jesus knew full well that His disciples wouldn't comprehend it all. Still, they were staggered by the impact of His words.

Tucked in with the hard words Jesus spoke was a nugget of good news which, ironically, didn't even penetrate the disciples' minds or make sense to these grief-stricken men at the time. "But I tell you the truth: It is for your good that I am going away. Unless I go away, the Counselor [the Holy Spirit] will not come to you" (v. 7).

How could it be? What did it all mean?

It would be days before these men had any answers, days filled with loneliness, fear and excruciating sorrow over the death of their Lord. Demoralized, they couldn't even recall—let alone believe—Jesus' promise of hope: "You will grieve, but your grief will turn to joy" (v. 20).

They hadn't counted on a miracle-working God, one who would grasp His Son from the grip of death, foiling Satan's plans. Jesus, the world's Redeemer, was alive and well! His words were true: He was with the Father. Then, as promised, He dispatched the Holy Spirit from heaven. Like a mighty, rushing wind, the Spirit came to fill their hearts at the Jewish festival of Pentecost in Jerusalem (see Acts 2:1-41).

Immediately, the once-cowering disciples began preaching in the streets of Jerusalem, boldly declaring that the resurrected Jesus was both Lord and Christ.

Courage! Empowerment! Joy so uninhibited it provoked onlookers to say, "They have had too much wine" (Acts 2:13). But they were not drunk. They were filled to overflowing with the Holy Spirit, and they could not keep quiet about their Lord.

Larry Christianson, Lutheran renewal leader, echoes this same fact. "From the day of Pentecost onward, the coming of the Spirit has been inseparably linked with telling people what God has done, is doing and will do through Christ and the giving of His Holy Spirit."[1]

"It is for your good that I am going away" (John 16:7). For our good? Yes!

The empowering of the Holy Spirit was normal and "good" for believers in the early church. Ignited by the living presence of Christ within them, they fearlessly proclaimed the gospel in all its power across Asia Minor, into Africa and Europe. This same Spirit continues to be poured out in our day, equipping us—His church—to carry God's message of hope and salvation into all the world.

At the turn of the twentieth century, the Lord poured out His Holy Spirit in a dramatic way in California in what came to be known as the Azusa Street Revival. Supernatural gifts of the Spirit were manifested everywhere—healings, tongues, prophecies. Many said it was the "work of the enemy," and that it would soon "blow over."

They were right. It blew all over the world.[2]

By 1960, the winds of the Holy Spirit were blowing in mainline churches. By 1967, the winds began to blow in the Roman Catholic church. By 1977, nearly all the denominations had been touched. From small beginnings in the early 1900s to the present day, this renewal has brought an estimated 411 million people around the world to a new experience in the Holy Spirit. And the result? Refreshment, revival and empowerment in the Body of Christ.

No wonder Jesus said that His leaving would be a good thing.

## A Personal Filling

I didn't know about the solid history of the Holy Spirit's work when I first listened that day in Burbank to my Lutheran friend's story about her baptism in the Holy Spirit.

However, on that Seattle morning in my kitchen, I knew that I was the Lord's child, that I now had a personal relationship with Jesus Christ. But, I also knew I had a lot to learn.

I discovered my sister-in-law had also had this experience with the Holy Spirit. She was a solid, mainline church member and a woman I well respected. I was still uncertain about this experience, yet I couldn't deny the change in her.

Others were talking about the power of the Holy Spirit for our day and about what was happening in mainline churches throughout the late '60s and early '70s. This was big news; numerous articles and books were being written on the subject. One book, *Nine O'Clock in the Morning* by Dennis Bennett, rector of St. Luke's Episcopal Church in Seattle, was especially helpful in clarifying for me the role of the Holy Spirit.

As I devoured this book, things began adding up for me. My fears were being dissipated under the gentle drawing I first felt that day in Burbank after my friend shared her experience.

I knew I had to get myself to the Friday night meeting at St. Luke's where Dennis Bennett talked about the baptism in the Holy Spirit. It was an appointment I needed to keep. I drove with a friend to the Ballard district, and we walked into St. Luke's, where we sat in the very back of the church.

I listened closely as Father Bennett talked about how the Holy Spirit was poured out at Pentecost. He not only described the events Luke recorded in the book of Acts, but he shared his own experience of being filled with the Holy Spirit and receiving the gift of tongues.

I'd never heard anything like what happened next. A man named Stanley gave a "message in tongues." It was beautiful, rhythmical, like someone speaking in another language.

Silence hung in the room for a few minutes. Then, a gray-haired lady named Edna stepped forward, faced the audience and gave the interpretation in English, speaking in the exact rhythmic pattern Stanley had spoken in.

This was the Holy Spirit. I knew it in the deepest part of my being. All my reservations dissolved.

I couldn't leave that meeting without going forward to be prayed for to receive the baptism of the Holy Spirit. Although my mouth was dry and my knees shook, I made my way to the altar and asked the Holy Spirit to fill me.

I waited as the others at the altar quietly began speaking in a heavenly language. But I had no such manifestation at the time. I walked away thinking, *It didn't happen to me. Maybe it won't happen to me.*

For several weeks, I struggled intellectually with my feelings about the gifts of the Spirit. *It this all for real? And are these gifts for our day?*

Some weeks later, in a phone conversation, a longtime friend strongly encouraged me. "Jane, you need to make a decision. Do you really believe this is true?"

My quick answer surprised me. "I believe it is true." I hung up the phone and went directly into my bedroom and began praying. Miraculously, a heavenly language came pouring from my lips. The heavens opened as I'd never experienced, bathing me in waves of the Father's love. I was vitally aware of the presence of Jesus in a new way.

My heart flooded over with the deep realization of being accepted, loved and forgiven. I didn't want to leave the room, but when I eventually stood to my feet, I remember saying, "Jesus, You are real."

## Walking in a New Dimension

After my experience with the Holy Spirit, I began to discover Christ's "good thing" dimension in my life.

This Jesus, whom I had heard about all my life, was no longer shrouded in the pages of my childhood Sunday School papers or hidden in the verses of an old gospel hymn.

He was real. Alive. A Friend. A Companion. A Loving Presence. Never in my life had I experienced anything like this—actually feeling Jesus' love and loving Him in return.

From the first moment I experienced the release of a heavenly prayer language, it was as if someone had turned on the light switch.

Prayer became easy and natural, like having an intimate conversation with a best friend. I had a hunger for God's Word in a way I had never experienced. The Word of God opened to me. Scripture I'd previously read came alive.

FOR THE FIRST TIME IN MY LIFE,
I SENSED THE THIRST IN MY SOUL AND
THE ACHE IN MY HEART DIMINISH.

Another extraordinary difference came, unannounced, almost as if through the back door: For the first time in my life, I sensed the thirst in my soul and the ache in my heart diminish.

How do you share such a tremendous spiritual experience?

Before I had time even to think about how I might tell Howard and the others around me, the Lord impressed me to be quiet for a time about what had happened.

## Sharing My Story

A year later, Howard and I were talking in our kitchen one evening as we finished dinner. I pushed back my chair and moved to the counter to cut our pie for dessert.

I filled our coffee cups and eased back into my chair. "Howie," I began, "I want to tell you something that happened to me awhile back...something really significant."

Howard put his fork down and looked expectantly across the table at me. Simply and directly, I told him about my experience with the Holy Spirit.

For a full minute, Howard said nothing. I waited for his response, feeling at once curious and at peace. When it came, it was tender and affirming. Again, here was strong evidence of the way the Holy Spirit comes alongside as a "helper."

"I don't understand it at all, Jane, but I'll tell you one thing," Howard said, "I can't deny the truth of it because of the change I see in you."

## The Word of the Hour

"Change" was the word of the hour. What happened to me in 1969 was happening to thousands of others experiencing the baptism in the Holy Spirit. Praise meetings, teaching tapes and Bible studies swept across the U.S. It was a season where faith was high and prayers seemed to be answered quickly as believers discovered the reality of a supernatural God.

By 1970, I was headed in a new direction. My schedule, priorities, my concerns all began to focus on a life where God was a living reality. I was energized by my new relationship with Jesus and by studying and teaching the Bethel Bible Study Series at church. Still, I hungered to know even more about the practical outworking of the Spirit-filled life.

In September of 1971, I invited Shade O'Driscoll, the co-rector's wife of St. Luke's Episcopal Church, to our home on a Thursday morning to share her testimony and bring her teaching on womanhood. Eight women came. Soon others were asking if they could also attend. The group grew. And grew.

"How many did you have today?" Invariably, Howard asked me for a count every Thursday night when he came home for dinner. We had agreed to open our home for whomever God would bring. But in our wildest imaginations, neither of us had any idea that this group would explode. Thirty-five to forty women came on a regular basis for two years.

Many days, sixty women would squeeze in. Occasionally, eighty, and once, a hundred women took up every inch of our living room. They came by word of mouth: friends, neighbors, friends of friends. Many Thursday mornings, I'd open the door and find complete strangers on my porch. And they all asked the same question: "Is this the house where someone is teaching a Bible study?"

Women drove across town to hear about the Holy Spirit and receive His gifts. Like hungry children, we were learning together how to walk in a new dimension.

## *My Aglow Beginnings*

One afternoon in 1972, a friend, Paula Shields, invited me to a home prayer meeting. Her invitation seemed a bit vague.

"What's this all about?" I quizzed her. "Does this group meet on a regular basis?" It was curious that, with my current associations with Christian women, I hadn't heard of a group called Aglow.

Paula was enthusiastic, but noncommittal, and I was interested enough to join her.

At the meeting, the prayer emphasis centered on finding new leadership for the Edmonds Aglow gathering. I sat, quietly enjoying my coffee and the fellowship, as the women counted the secret ballots. When they finished, one woman gave the verdict: "Jane, you'll be the new Edmonds Aglow president."

I nearly dropped my coffee in my lap. "Me? You've got to be kidding!"

The very thought of standing in front of people made my stomach queasy. It wasn't that I didn't want to be available to the Lord; it was that this would involve me in an area for which I knew I had no natural giftings. I simply couldn't do it.

"I have trouble praying in front of others," I stammered. "I'm the one who quit speech class in high school."

My protestations, however, didn't deter these women. Sensing my shock and apprehension, they immediately gathered around me, laid hands on me and prayed. One by one, they promised their support. While they insisted they'd been led by the Holy Spirit to choose me, I jokingly told them later that it felt more like "holy arm twisting"!

Knowing I was unfamiliar with Aglow, Paula shared the history and vision of the group with me. It began in 1967, when four Seattle women met to seek the Lord about forming a group that would provide interdenominational Christian fellowship for women. By 1972, it had incorporated with sixty fellowships established across the United States. Neither Paula nor I knew at the time that God would provide stunning growth for Aglow in those next few years. Aglow boards would be established in Canada, Israel, Australia, India, the Netherlands, Mexico, New Zealand, Nigeria, Kenya and Ghana.

Surprisingly, Aglow was born in north Seattle, not far from where I now lived. Soon after, another group formed in Edmonds, a little seaside town north of Seattle. Drawing twenty-five to thirty women to a restaurant every month, the group gave women a chance to worship the Lord and share testimonies of what God was doing by His Spirit.

## What Now?

As the new president of Edmonds Aglow, I considered the immediate future.

My co-leader and I met together the next day, but we hadn't the faintest idea where to start. So we prayed.

We agreed to start by finding a meeting place. We wanted an attractive room where women would feel comfortable coming for lunch and inviting friends to join them. We finally found a spot on the waterfront overlooking Puget Sound and the Olympic Mountains. The manager was interested in having us—even without charge. But there was one catch: We had to guarantee that at least 100 women would come.

Faith often feels foolish. And it did that day.

We had no money, but I turned to the manager and said, "We promise you one hundred women."

Our new board, meeting for the first time at my home, prayed earnestly for women to come to our first Aglow meeting in the new place. Much to our utter astonishment, on the day of the luncheon, more than 100 women came!

For the next two years, the Edmonds group had a flourishing life of its own. It was rare that they had less than 125 women. Sometimes as many as 350 women came to worship and fellowship in the power of the Holy Spirit—and to hear a variety of speakers share the Word of the Lord.

## Trusting God's Voice

During the time I was president of the Edmonds group in 1972, I also agreed to fill out the term of the recording secretary at the recently established Aglow headquarters office in Edmonds.

I finished the term for recording secretary and went on to be vice president of Washington State Aglow for a year. It was a good time, a time of growth and learning, but I sensed the Lord taking me in a new direction, and when I was asked to commit to another year of leadership, I declined. I sensed so strongly that the Lord was saying to me, "Come away, my beloved; spend time with me."

The selection committee, however, was persistent. "Jane, we have prayed and fasted and everyone on our committee still comes up with your name. Won't you reconsider?"

Their reasoning was persuasive, and I did not want to miss the Lord's true leading. At the same time, I couldn't dismiss the inner "No" I kept hearing. A tug of war ensued, mostly inside me.

Thinking I had misunderstood the voice inside me, I called my dad for counsel. He and Mother had recently retired to Edmonds and we enjoyed a wonderful closeness with each other, appreciating all the Lord had done in healing our hearts. I knew I could trust Dad's counsel.

"Am I hearing right, Dad? All the women on the committee insist that the Lord has given them my name."

Dad's voice was warm and assuring. "Honey, God wants you to hear His voice above all others. Trust what you hear Him saying to you." And I did.

## A Season of Servanthood

Excused from Aglow leadership, and back home in my comfort zone, I had no obligations except for family.

The kids were busy in school, Howard was traveling some and I had days to myself to read, pray and do the creative things that gave me pleasure: baking, gardening, a little redecorating.

One day, I phoned a friend who'd attended the prayer meetings in my home. Frances was a lovely woman, confined to a wheelchair with multiple sclerosis. She mentioned that she needed someone to help her three days a week, but she wanted the woman to be a Christian.

Frances hadn't finished talking when I felt clearly impressed with the words, "You're the one, Jane." Part of the urge was financial. I'd been looking anxiously at an account I needed to pay off and this seemed like an opportunity. But much more than that, I sensed it was the Lord's leading.

Frances lived in a beautiful Tudor home, tucked back among a grove of evergreen trees above Puget Sound. I was with her three days a week for a year and a half. Totally responsible for all her personal care, I also fixed lunch, started dinner and did the laundry as well as light housekeeping.

None of it was drudgery.

A few months prior to this job, I'd heard a speaker share on servanthood at an Aglow area retreat. I remember leaving that meeting pondering the subject: What does it really mean to be a servant?

Not so long after that, my answer came. In the midst of drying Frances's feet after her morning bath, I heard the tender, quiet voice of the Holy Spirit: "Jane, I am teaching you to have the heart of a servant."

## *How Could They Understand?*

Like so many of life's valuable experiences, my working for Frances wasn't totally understood by those around me. Howard kiddingly called me his "little domestic." Friends were sincerely puzzled about "Jane's job," and were determined to get a satisfactory explanation from me.

"I can't believe you're doing this," was the usual opening gambit. "Since when did you decide to become a maid?"

I had no answers for their ears. How could I communicate the inexplicable joy of ministering to my friend? Telling them I was "on assignment from the Lord" sounded almost foolish, coming from a woman with a comfortable home in the suburbs and a husband with a good job.

GOD WAS FITTING ME FOR AN INTERNAL
WARDROBE CHANGE. GRADUALLY THE HEAVY
CLOTHES WERE TAKEN OFF UNTIL ONE
DAY, I WAS DASHING ABOUT, LIGHT AS
A BALLERINA IN A CHIFFON DRESS.

Alone much of the time, Frances was spiritually hungry and eagerly awaited my arrival each morning. Amazingly, I was just as eager to come. It was as if our hearts were being knit together as we interacted during the daily schedule that made up her routine.

I started each day by giving her exercises for her legs and feet. We followed with her bath. After I dressed her, the highlight of the day was our fellowship, sharing the Lord and praying together. Those shared moments were what God spontaneously produced between us throughout the day.

Something else was happening inside me, however. It was as if I were being fitted for an internal wardrobe change. At first I felt as if I were walking around bundled up in a heavy wool coat, clutching my scarf to my neck, but gradually the heavy clothes were taken off until one day, I suddenly realized that I was dashing about, light as a ballerina in a chiffon dress.

The more I poured myself out to serve Frances, the less I cared what other people thought of me. The facade of acceptability that I'd built around myself and my family began to disintegrate.

This was not the stuff of great spiritual revelation. It was simply something I was walking through, an interlude in my life in which God was teaching me abundant lessons in humility as well as deeply satisfying me with the joy of serving.

My year and a half with Frances flew by.

On my last day with her, we said our tearful good-byes. As I walked to my car, a verse from John's Gospel whispered to my heart, "I no longer call you [servant]....Instead, I have called you [friend]" (John 15:15).

I started the car and looked back at the brilliant purple heather blooming along the driveway of Frances's lovely home. All I could say as I pulled out was, "Thank you, Lord."

## A New Family Crisis

My life was full of a growing awareness of the Holy Spirit and His power—and a newfound joy in being with others who were also learning to walk in the Spirit.

But life was not perfect. There were still problems in our home. In fact, one of them was escalating.

None of us realized at the time how traumatic our move from California in 1969 had been for my son, Jeff. Like my brother,

Jimmy, who left his friends and relationships back in Akron, Jeff left behind friends he had grown close to during our four years in California. Finding his niche with the kids in his new school in Edmonds proved difficult for a sixth grader heading into puberty, with all its physical and emotional upheaval.

Jeff's sixth-grade teacher noted that he was struggling. "Jeff's a tenderhearted boy. With his sensitivity, I can see how he easily feels frustrated and defeated. Then, to compensate, he becomes the class clown. It's typical of kids his age to want their peers' acceptance."

Unfortunately, Jeff's search for approval eventually led to his "hanging around" with kids who were also struggling with feeling good about themselves—and who were experimenting with smoking and dressing in counterculture style.

Jeff began bringing home poor report cards, or skipping school altogether. Associating with at-loose-ends kids, his behavior alarmed us all. But it was especially tough on Howard. He and Jeff were colliding at almost every turn.

During those years, Howard reacted strongly. He instinctively did what he knew to do from his own father: He tightened the reins.

The stricter Howard became, the more Jeff resisted. Jeff continued to drift closer to his "tough guy" friends.

By high school, Jeff was in full-blown rebellion. Hair down to his shoulders, headbands, ratty jackets and torn jeans were his rebellious label. He looked and acted like the prototype hard rocker of the 1970s.

As Jeff's mother, I was beside myself with worry. I was caught in the middle between Jeff and Howard, believing Howard's approach to discipline was too severe.

At the same time, I felt Howard didn't realize the extent of the situation. I was sure that Jeff was on drugs. "There's more to this than the ordinary teenage rebellion," I told Howard, pleading with him to consider the possibility.

"He'll be all right, Jane," Howard countered. "He just needs some good, old-fashioned discipline." Like so many fathers,

Howard couldn't bring himself to see such problems in his own son. His solution was denial, anger and more rules.

Nothing anyone did stemmed the tide of Jeff's downward spiral. By his junior year, he dropped out of high school altogether. Now, clearly on marijuana, other drugs and alcohol, he was in and out of the house, out sometimes for days at a time—whereabouts unknown.

In the meantime, the rest of us were being torn apart by the confusion and tension this kind of behavior breeds. Any way you looked at it, we were living a nightmare. I was sick with worry, Howard manifested his worry in anger, and Lisa and Scott were two scared kids.

## A Night to Remember

In July of 1975, Howard and I, along with Lisa and Scott, took a ten-day trip in a motor home with family friends from California. Together, we headed up to Banff and Lake Louise to vacation in the beautiful Canadian Rockies. Because Jeff was working, we felt comfortable leaving him at home.

Making good time on our return trip, we arrived home several hours earlier than we expected. I walked up to the front porch, put my key in the lock, opened the door, and stepped into a darkened house with all the drapes pulled.

That undeniable, sickly sweet smell hit me full force in the face. Marijuana. I wanted to scream out every ounce of breath I'd ever taken in. I covered my mouth with one hand; with the other, I groped for the light switch. I needed a steadying hand. "Howard, please come quick!"

Alarmed at my tone, Howard ran past our friends and stopped next to me in the entrance hall. Lisa and Scott squeezed by us, their mouths falling open at the disaster before them in the living room. "Look at your chair, Mom," Scott said, running to lift the overstuffed chair that was on its side next to an overturned lamp.

Howard, now in action, carefully checked out the rest of the house. I stood still in the entrance hall, unable to move further.

By now, Scott had reported the beer bottles and cigarette burns on the coffee table. Lisa yelled from downstairs, "I can't even open the laundry room door. It's piled too high with people's dirty clothes."

Howard stalked back to my side, his body trembling with anger. "Jane, somebody threw up on our bed!"

My stomach turned and my knees went weak. I whirled around to Howard and buried my head in his chest. I couldn't believe Jeff would allow this to happen. "Oh, Howie, we've been through so much with this kid." I was utterly undone.

## A Cry for Help

Hours later, after the house had been aired, vacuumed and scrubbed, I dropped into bed. A light knock sounded at our bedroom door.

It was Lisa, standing in her nightgown. Her blue eyes wide open, she looked at my face with great sadness. I pulled her over to sit closely on my side of the bed and started gently rubbing her back. "Pretty tough homecoming, Lisa."

Tears trickled down her cheeks. She turned her head toward me, her eyes briefly searching mine for answers. "Mom, how could Jeff do this to us?"

Reaching for lotion on the nightstand, I continued to stroke her back and neck. I told her the truth. "Jeff's behavior is a cry for help, Lisa. He needs it desperately In fact, we all do."

She was silent for a minute, allowing me to stroke away some of the hurt she felt. Then I felt her back muscles tense again. "Lisa," I said, "it's going to be okay."

Okay? I hadn't the faintest idea what we could do. I was at my wit's end.

Howard and I still couldn't talk openly about it. We couldn't seem to connect at the heart level, let alone pray together over the problem. It was obvious that we had a grave situation on our hands. Everyone in the family was hurting, and I was the hand-wringing mother, terrified of the effects of Jeff's wrong choices. I saw him as a confused teenager, smoking, drinking and drugging his days away, falling prey to the attacks of Satan.

Was I going to lose my son?

## A New Dimension in Prayer

One afternoon, as I finished grocery shopping, I was aware of an intense heaviness of spirit. I walked to my car, loaded the bags in the back seat and drove home. Words are inadequate to describe the sorrow that rose up deep within me that day. This was a wrenching, all-consuming heartbrokenness.

No one was home when I pulled in. I walked directly upstairs to our bedroom, went into our walk-in closet and closed the door. I had to be alone in a place where I could physically groan.

Unsure of what was happening in me, I calmly took authority over any activity of Satan. Then I said, "Lord, I yield to you."

I waited...and waited.

From the pit of my insides, a weeping welled up in me that was unlike any weeping I'd ever experienced. It burst forth in deep, inarticulate groans, giving expression to the agony within me.

I wailed over my family. "Oh, God, come and establish Your kingdom in our home." Those were the only words I spoke, and I repeated them over and over, the burden of my soul coming forth with more groaning and travail.

I don't know how long I was in my closet that day. All I know was that I felt like a woman in her first labor. She doesn't know what to expect, but her time has come and there is no turning back. I had no alternative but to give myself to this work—for days and weeks to come.

Most days my praying began with this same deep weeping. I cried out my petitions to God, speaking aloud for all of my family: "Oh, God, establish Your throne in Howard's heart. Protect Lisa and Scott from any ungodly influence. Turn Jeff's heart back to You."

I declared to the enemy that he had gone this far and he could go no further in the Hansen household. I spoke out strongly in the name of Jesus: "I push back the forces of darkness and I call forth light!" To mark that declaration, I went to my front door and to every doorpost in the house, anointing each one with oil. In faith, I called forth "things that are not as though they were" (Rom. 4:13).

My confidence grew as I yielded up every member of my family to God and declared His promises over them. And where Jeff was concerned, I prayed, "Lord, I release him to You. I don't just want a young man who is cleaned up and off drugs. Do whatever You have to do to bring forth a man of God."

One day during this time, a Scripture passage, one that I'd heard spoken by internationally known teacher Jack Hayford, came to me special delivery like a set of instructions: "Sing, O barren woman, you who never bore a child; burst into song, shout for joy, you who were never in labor, because more are the children of the desolate woman than of her who has a husband" (Isa. 54:1).

After that day, I began to sing to the spiritually barren areas in our family and invite the Holy Spirit to have authority over our home. "Enlarge the place of your tent, stretch your tent curtains wide. Do not fear disgrace; you will not be humiliated" (Isa. 54:2,4).

I spoke God's promises aloud as I worked around the house, dismantling the "barrenness" by faith and calling forth fruitfulness.

Of course, I was a woman of prayer, but before this time, I never considered myself an intercessor. I always thought that intercessors were "a select few" who closeted themselves away on big assignments from God.

In retrospect, I can see that I didn't just wake up one day and decide to pray for my family. Without a doubt, a "spirit of intercession" had come upon me. God, by His Holy Spirit, did something outside myself.

Would I ever know the results of this prayer?

Yes, that day would come. At the time, however, obedience was the issue. Still, in the next few months, I witnessed many hopeful signs that fruit was growing within our family.

## Howard's Heart

During the next few years, I could see the Holy Spirit drawing Howard to Jesus. Through a couples' fellowship in our home, a dramatic deliverance from a long-entrenched smoking habit and a miraculous healing of phlebitis while hospitalized, God, in His creative timing, wooed Howard to Himself.

While on a business trip to Montana, he read a book by Don Basham, a popular teacher and writer now deceased. The words touched him in a deep, personal way. Alone in a car, he pulled off the road and called out to God. Howard surrendered his life to Him, saying, "I want whatever You have for me."

Even though as a young boy he had a meaningful, spiritual experience when he was confirmed in the Lutheran church, he had never lived in the light of that experience. That night in Montana was Howard's point of conversion.

Two days later, while he was driving to Cody, Wyoming, he began to pray aloud, asking Jesus to baptize him with the Holy Spirit. To his utter amazement a new language began to come forth. He knew it was the beginning of a new walk with the Lord.

He called me immediately to share the "good news." The moment I picked up the phone, I heard excitement in Howard's voice. "Jane, guess what happened to me this afternoon? You won't believe it!"

But I did believe it! Right in the middle of cowboy country, the Holy Spirit had rounded up Howard. What jubilant news! Our family was headed into a new dimension.

Howard's taste of the Spirit's presence in such a profound way gave me a new sense of thanksgiving. I remembered my own experience of the loving presence of Jesus drawing me to Himself, filling me with no less than His supernatural life.

But there was more.

God was at work to bring healing and wholeness to Howard, to me and to our entire family. In His immense love, He wanted to teach me first about obedience and servanthood. Now I was learning to be His warrior/intercessor over my home and loved ones. Only after these lessons had been learned would I be able to understand the next one.

I was about to enter one of the greatest, most difficult instructional periods of my life as I became a student/patient with the Master Teacher. This period of instruction would require me to submit my heart to the Master Surgeon for radical surgery, despite the pain.

Finally, I was ready.

CHAPTER SIX

$\mathcal{G}$OING FOR THE $\mathcal{H}$EART

The Bible is filled with stories of people with flawed hearts. People who made mistakes, who told lies, who didn't raise their children well. Think about these Old Testament individuals: a patriarch whose cowardice caused his wife to be given for a king's pleasure; a brother who deceived his father to gain his blessing; a man, groomed to be the leader of the Israelite nation, whose hot temper led him to kill an Egyptian in anger; a king who committed adultery and tried to cover it with murder.

The New Testament stories are just as graphic: a disciple whose bravado gives way to betrayal; followers of Jesus who squabble over being first; a woman caught in adultery; another oppressed with demon spirits. As Bible teacher Dr. Herbert Lockyer has said, "Sinners by birth become, more or less, sinners by practice."[1]

Spiritually flawed hearts can only be repaired by the Master Surgeon, just as physically damaged hearts demand attention from an experienced cardiologist.

An early Seattle pioneer in pediatric and adult heart surgery—and an outspoken man of faith—Dr. Lester Sauvage gave a newspaper interview shortly after his retirement. "The human heart beats 40 million times a year," he said. "By the time you're 25 years old, it has beat about one billion times, working in a tireless manner to propel nourishment to every one of the 60 trillion cells in the body."[2]

This man, who has seen 4,000 to 5,000 human hearts, who has studied and repaired them, still speaks of them with awe. "You know when you look at things like this that there has to be a God."[3]

Belgian cardiologist Dr. Noubar Boyadjian notes in his book, *The Heart,* "Since the beginning of time, the heart has been the symbol of the most precious thing the human race possesses: love...the most intimate central point of the human person."[4]

Love. The heart. Even flawed hearts.

When human beings shy away from those whose hearts are in pain, Jesus comes to us in our need, confident in His ability to bring forth health and thus allow our hearts to function as they were intended.

Jesus offered His understanding heart to notorious sinners who approached Him. He allowed women to touch Him with their gifts of adoration—without a word of condemnation. He looked at their hearts. His mission was to forgive and to heal hearts broken in shame and hardened by wrong choices. By the power of His shed blood, He is still doing that today.

I know, because that's what He did for me.

## The Symptoms Surface

How does a good little girl like me end up needing heart surgery? Just as years of cholesterol buildup, bad dietary habits, smoking and stress will eventually damage a physical heart, the years of undealt-with hurt in my heart gradually turned to anger as surely as cholesterol blocks arteries.

None of this happens overnight. It's progressive. Insidiously so. My hurt would go underground for long periods of time. Then, a situation, a remark, a disappointment would act like a bellows over a dying fire, infusing it with enough oxygen to burn all day. That's what mine did; it burst into flames of anger.

If you'd seen me in my home, you might have wanted to protest this description because I could function so well. The atmosphere in our home was congenial. Howard and I entertained friends, kept busy with the kids, and life went on.

But beneath the surface, I had become a boiling pot filled with anger. Hurt from my marriage merged with the hurt from my childhood that never stopped telling me, "There's no time for you; you're unlovable."

Hurt undealt with becomes anger. Undealt-with anger becomes bitterness.

## Flashpoint

One Saturday morning, as Howard and I finished repotting our deck baskets, I opened up with my same old battery of questions. "Why can't I seem to connect with you, Howie? What is this unseen wall between us?"

The pain of my loneliness prodded me on that morning, and I pushed the old issue out again. "Why do you keep yourself so hidden from me?"

Head down, holding a hose to flush off the walk under the deck, Howard ignored my questions. Instead of answering, he said, "If we don't get this moss off the concrete, we'll have to get someone in here with a jackhammer to break this stuff up."

*Jackhammer!* His words hit me like a slap. I stormed into the house, kicked off my yard shoes and flung my garden gloves across the kitchen table. *Easy enough for you to understand how to break up cement,* I thought, *but I can't seem to pound anything into your head about us, no matter how hard I try.* Howard followed me into the kitchen, our raised voices reverberating throughout the house.

These little explosions always subsided after awhile, but more and more my anger was seeping out at the edges. I couldn't keep it in any longer. Too many years of trying to please, trying not to rock the boat, had gone by. The obedient child. The nice wife. I'd had too many years of feeling as if no one cared or even heard.

Resentment filled me to overflowing. Just like the person needing heart surgery, the day comes when you need help so badly, you don't care how much it hurts because nothing can hurt worse than what you're experiencing.

That's where I was.

Everything was out of control in our home. An alcoholic and drug-addicted son, two other hurting children and a marriage that was sifting like sand through my fingers meant we were on our way to the emotional emergency room. Howard and I had to get help.

One day, I stood in front of the bathroom mirror and said, "I can't deal with this pain and anger any longer. Someone has got to listen to me."

## *Appointment with Truth*

Several friends of mine had sought help from a pastor and his wife, a woman about my age, who had a wonderful counseling ministry in a rural church north of us. On my friends' strong recommendation, I phoned Dick and Marilyn Williamson for an appointment.

"Dick," I blurted out, "I feel like a boiling pot, filled with anger and rage. I can't keep the lid on any longer, and it all seems focused on my husband."

We set an appointment and I hung up the phone.

Scripture is quick to acknowledge anger as a normal human emotion—and equally quick to warn of its potential danger if left undealt with. Paul's words to the believers at Ephesus are a case in point:

When angry, do not sin; do not ever let your wrath (your exasperation, your fury or indignation) last until the sun goes down. Leave no [such] room or foothold for the devil [give no opportunity to him] (Eph. 4:26,27, *Amp.*).

According to Dr. Larry Crabb, Christian psychologist and author, "Anger tells us something about ourselves that deserves attention, something that will need to be exposed and changed before we can move along the path to mature love."[5]

In the story of Cain and Abel, we see the classic illustration of runaway, unrepentant anger and its tragic consequences. Angry that the Lord accepted Abel's offering and rejected his, Cain's reaction was written all over his face.

Then the Lord said to Cain, "Why are you angry? Why is your face downcast? If you do what is right, will you not be accepted?" (Gen. 4:6,7).

At that point, Cain had the perfect opportunity to deal with his anger. He could have approached the Lord and his brother in humility and conquered his raging feelings, as well as gained their acceptance.

God even spelled out the danger of retaining anger. "But if you do not do what is right, sin is crouching at your door; it desires to have you, but you must master it" (Gen. 4:7).

Closed off to repentance and reconciliation, Cain let his anger rule him. His rampaging emotions carried him swiftly into a violent act of revenge.

Now Cain said to his brother Abel, "Let's go out to the field." And while they were in the field, Cain attacked his brother Abel and killed him (Gen. 4:8).

From anger, to hatred, to murder.

Does it seem like a gargantuan leap? The First Epistle of John clearly reinforces this progression of undealt-with anger, again using Cain's life as an example: "Anyone who hates his brother is a murderer, and you know that no murderer has eternal life in him" (1 John 3:15).

When confronted with Scripture, I could no longer hide my anger nor dismiss it as just another natural emotion. I was, in fact, a perfect example of a woman whose anger was spiraling downward toward hatred.

## Surgery Begins

This is exactly the condition I was in when Howard and I arrived at the Williamsons' house. Although Howard and I were both smiling on the outside, I was boiling inside. Undoubtedly, Dick and Marilyn could see beyond my pretense, but their warm, opening words accepted me without qualification: "How can we help you two?"

We sat together around their table. I started to speak, "Well, we really have problems...." My lip quivered. I sighed deeply into the expectant stillness. Then I could no longer hold the feelings back. A torrent of tears broke loose.

"Let it go, Jane," Marilyn encouraged, as she extended a box of tissues to me. I did. I grabbed a tissue and went ahead, pouring out my frustrations in our marriage, barely stopping for breath as my words tumbled over each other.

All the time I was speaking, Howard rocked back and forth, nervously trying to look as if he didn't have a care in the world.

Looking back now, it must have been obvious to the Williamsons that we were both in extreme pain, covering and protecting ourselves with different strategies. Until recently, I'd hidden my pain and anger beneath a "can-do" exterior. Howard's cover was to joke and laugh, hoping to convince himself and others that he really did have life under control.

Now, however, all pretense gone, I emotionally communicated to the Williamsons how hard I had worked at our marriage through the years. I was not so overwrought that I couldn't see the real solution to this problem: Howard needed to change.

## Why Me?

In the sessions that followed, Dick Williamson directed most of his comments to me, because I was the one who seemed most eager for answers. Once, Dick looked at me and made an observation that hit me as obvious: "Jane, you're looking to Howard to get your needs met."

I could feel the defensiveness rise up in me. "Of course I'm expecting Howard to meet my needs," I snapped. "That's why I'm so angry. After all, what is marriage about, anyway?"

His questioning confused me. I just wanted to move on, to get to the "real counseling," the part where Dick could realize, and authoritatively point out, that Howard was responsible for our problems. But Dick kept addressing me.

*Why isn't he talking to Howard?* I thought, as I sat there.

I came away from those first sessions puzzled and irritated. *Why was Howard always getting off the hook?* I questioned. *Why are the sessions so focused on me, my expectations, my judgments, my anger?*

I thought I'd made my case pretty clear. I couldn't understand how Dick and Marilyn, so experienced in counseling, could fail to recognize the problem and tell Howard what to do so our marriage could be turned around.

Finally at one session, I remember feeling pleased when Dick challenged Howard on his tendency to defuse serious moments with laughter and jokes. "Is everything funny to you, Howard?" he asked.

Howard was silent as Dick settled back in his chair for what seemed like a long period of silence. Only the steady ticking of the clock invaded the heavy moment.

Then Dick shifted forward again, laid his arms on the table and leaned toward Howard as he asked quietly, "Howard, tell me about your relationship with Jesus."

Howard cleared his throat. Then he smiled at Dick, trying to look comfortable with the notion that he'd been tossed a question he could answer. "My dad was a pastor," he began, "I've been baptized and confirmed." He added, "We were always in church."

"I hear you, Howard. But I'm asking about relationship. What's your relationship with Jesus?"

JESUS WOULD NOT BE THWARTED BY THE FEAR THAT HELD A STRANGLEHOLD ON ONE TALL, BLOND TRAVEL AGENT'S HEART. HE WOULD KEEP REACHING OUT.

I held my breath. No one had ever pressed Howard about the issue of relationship with Jesus.

Indeed, Howard had accepted Jesus as his Savior, but it seemed as though his relationship with the Lord reflected the same pattern as his relationship with me and others—emotionally closed. Because of this, his relationship with the Lord seemed to be hindered as well.

Dick's question triggered a deep fear in Howard that he had reacted to with sarcasm many times in the past. He voiced it again now.

"What do you want me to be, a psalm singer?" Howard shifted uncomfortably. "I'm not going to be like one of these guys who go around looking pious. That's not for me."

"I understand where you are," Dick answered.

Little did Howard know that Dick had the same abhorrence

for phoniness and pretended piety. So did Jesus. But Jesus would
not be thwarted by the fear that had a stranglehold on one tall,
blond travel agent's heart. He would keep reaching out.

Dick turned back to me and posed a question I was to hear
more than once: "Why do you want Howard to change, Jane?"

## Points of Change

His question pushed me at a sensitive pressure point. The answer
seemed self-evident.

"What is marriage, anyway, if it isn't two people meeting
each other's needs? Even the Bible talks about husbands loving
their wives like Christ loved the Church."

I could explain my point of view, but I couldn't explain what
was happening to me; things were beginning to crumble inside.
"Why do you want Howard to change?" Dick's question kept
reverberating through my mind.

Now, for days after our counseling sessions, I felt weak and
vulnerable, as if something inside me was giving way. Like the
patient in the operating room, it was my turn for heart repair.

## Uncovering Wrong Beliefs

After several sessions with Dick and Marilyn, I began to notice a
pattern in how Dick confronted me. It closely resembled the
stance of a prosecuting attorney in court.

"Jane," he said, "you believe your husband should love you in
the way you want to be loved. When he doesn't, you become
self-protective and angry."

Pow! My head spun. I'd come to Dick and Marilyn to present
my case and here I was being treated as if I were the guilty one.

Before I could defend myself, Dick continued. "Doesn't God's
Word say, 'Whoever hates his brother is walking in darkness'?
How can you say that you have a relationship with God when you

hate your brother? After all, your relationship with your brother is only a picture of your relationship with God."

Everything in me wanted to marshal an army of convincing words to verbally defend myself. I'd never before had this belief buffeted by Scripture—without room for exceptions. "Isn't it true, Jane, that Jesus said we were to lay down our lives for our brother?" Dick asked.

"But I have," I protested. "I've encouraged Howard to communicate. I've kept a good house, paid the bills, gardened, kept up the yard." I paused for breath. "I've done everything I could to keep things going at home."

Dick's response flew back like a fastball. "Well, that's not necessarily laying down your life. That's doing 'things' for people and still keeping your real self closed and distanced from them."

I found myself bristling.

Surely I knew something about Scripture. I'd been raised in a pastor's home and attended Sunday School faithfully ever since I could remember. Furthermore, since my experience with the Holy Spirit, I'd been devouring Scripture, often for hours a day.

Still, I was now being challenged left and right. I could identify with the poor defendant scrambling to justify his actions as Dick pointed out, one by one, that my beliefs didn't line up with what the Bible said.

"When the Bible says, 'What you sow, you reap,' that applies to anger," Dick explained. "Jane, if you sow anger, you'll reap anger."

My response was instant. "But that doesn't feel fair. Howard's not doing his part. He has some responsibility in this marriage, too." I could feel the blood rush to my face and my fist tighten in my lap.

"Indeed he does," Dick nodded. "The call on the man's life is clearly stated in Scripture: 'Husbands, love your wives, just as Christ loved the church and gave himself up for her' (Eph. 5:25). But remember, no one can make him fulfill his side of the marriage contract. And, at the same time, his failure doesn't excuse you from loving him."

Finally, I looked at Dick and sighed. "You sure go for the throat, don't you?" He let my comment stand as if he hadn't heard me.

Then Marilyn spoke up. "Jane, often when we read the Word, we read the man's part where it outlines the husband's responsibility. You need to remember that we are responsible before God for only our part.

"The fact is that Scripture is unequivocal on this point. That's what Jesus taught in the Sermon on the Mount: Believers are called to love and walk in fellowship with our brothers and sisters, even when they do not love in return."*

I grew limp. This was more than a little debate. This was the Cross at work, slashing through my rights, my self-protection, my sense of fairness, my me-centered agenda. *Love when you are not loved in return? Love in the midst of pain? This would call us to an impossible task.* The very thought of it felt like death.

## Truth in the Silence

Neither Dick nor Marilyn said another word. We sat in silence. It was obvious the counseling session was over for the day. I had plenty to think about.

Just as I stood to reach for my coat, Dick made one last comment: "By the way, Jane, I don't go for the throat. I go for the heart."

For the first time since we'd come to counseling, Howard and I drove home in total silence. I, who always noticed the towering evergreens along the winding road above Puget Sound, made no mention of the fresh green tips of spring's new growth. We didn't even stop at McDonald's for our usual cup of coffee.

Within minutes of pulling into our driveway, Howard scooted up the stairs to read the newspaper. I headed straight for my

---

* *I'm not suggesting that a woman in an abusive situation remain in that circumstance. She should seek the help of a counselor or pastor qualified in abuse counseling.*

bedside Bible and brought it to the kitchen table. I had to see for myself what Scripture said about love.

I opened to the book of First John. The words stood out on the page like neon signs, heralding descriptions of God's love. I'd read all these verses many times, but they'd never impacted me like this.

Through the counseling process, I was seeing not only the anger, but the hatred in my own heart. Now, with my heart open and willing to look at and admit honestly what was really there, the truth of the Scriptures was coming alive to me in a new way.

I read and wept and wept and read.

Revelation. Enlightenment. Scales falling from my eyes.

I was seeing truth. It was reaching me at the heart level. The contrast of light and darkness was unmistakable. "Anyone who claims to be in the light but hates his brother is still in the darkness" (1 John 2:9). Relationship! The concept permeated every chapter.

"Anyone who hates his brother is a murderer, and you know that no murderer has eternal life in him" (1 John 3:15). No compromises, no exceptions in this passage.

"If anyone says, 'I love God,' yet hates his brother, he is a liar" (1 John 4:20). These weren't wishy-washy words or mealy-mouthed phrases. They were strong, definitive and absolute. Hater. Murderer. Liar.

Here I was, reading about the one basic of the Christian faith—love—and because I was honestly opening my heart, I saw myself in a new light: I was totally wrong. "Whoever does not love does not know God, because God is love" (1 John 4:8). Nothing here was contingent on the other person's loving me in return.

Dick's words haunted me: "Why do you want Howard to change?" I knew the case was ended. My defense was demolished.

## Moment of Truth

An epic moment of truth surfaced, one I will never forget. Now I knew the answer to Dick's question, but the words stuck in my throat. I hated to speak them, even in the quiet of my kitchen.

Why did I want Howard to change? My head bent, my heart open, I whispered, "For me! For me! For me! To meet my needs. For my happiness." I wanted change, not for Howard or even for God, but for Jane.

For the first time in my life, I saw the depth of my own sin, my own desperate need for change. "It's me, O Lord, standing in the need of prayer. Not my brother, not my sister, but me."

As painful as the counseling process was, I would no longer resist the scalpel of truth.

The next time the four of us met, I gave Dick and Marilyn complete freedom. "Hold back nothing," I said. "Leave no stone unturned. Tell me the truth. I want to be free."

Although Howard was apparently not as in touch with his pain as I was with mine at that point, he was willing to continue our counseling.

## Cutting Deeper

Dick and Marilyn's goal in counseling was to help me identify what I actually believed. This "battering on beliefs" had to be the starting point, because we live our lives out of what we hold to be true in our hearts.

It is not what we think or know in our minds, but what our hearts are convinced of that directs and guides our lives.

We all build our lives on premises—beliefs that we form and that "work" for us. These may be ideas we've learned in school, at home or even ones we've "caught" unconsciously as children from those we look up to. They're wordless expressions—a look on a face, an attitude shown in a certain situation—but they help shape our beliefs.

Brick by brick, we bring these beliefs into our impressionable minds, building the foundation upon which we live our lives.

Our behavior will give evidence that some of our heart-held

beliefs are wrong. We accept them as true and they are not. Is it any wonder we eventually run amok in our relationships with God and with those around us?

Dick kept probing at my flawed heart, ferreting out the wrong beliefs on which I'd based my life and exposing the angry responses that followed as a result.

Sometimes the scalpel of his words hit the artery of self-righteousness called *pride*, and I would begin to bleed. Then Marilyn would come alongside and clarify the direction we were going.

"Jane," she asked one day, "what do you get when you squeeze an orange?"

An obvious question, I thought.

She pursued her illustration. "You get orange juice because that's what's inside the orange. In your relationship with Howard, you are being squeezed. And what comes out of you? Anger!"

For an instant, my heart sank again. *Who wouldn't get angry?* But before I could protest, Dick picked up Marilyn's point.

"Howard can't make you angry, Jane. No one has that kind of control over another person. Your feelings are your feelings. They are a barometer of what you believe in your heart, and that's what's causing your distress."

"It's a sin problem, Jane."

That word again. Exactly the lesson I had begun to learn at the kitchen table recently. Dick leaned back in his chair, giving opportunity for his words to sink in. I could feel the Master Surgeon at work, "dividing soul and spirit, joints and marrow" (Heb. 4:12).

## Successful Surgery

Remarkably, during the next weeks at home, the Holy Spirit seemed to have a new kind of access to me. He expanded, clarified and confirmed where in the Bible I had missed the truth.

One day, Jesus' words in Matthew gripped me with a startling awareness of my condition:

"But whatever comes out of the mouth comes from the heart, and this is what makes a man unclean and defiles [him]. For out of the heart come evil thoughts (reasoning and disputings and designs) such as murder, adultery, sexual vice, theft, false witnessing, slander, and irreverent speech. These are what make a man unclean and defile [him]" (Matt. 15:18-20, *Amp.*).

I had never considered that what was spewing out of me—my boiling anger—was not just being unlovingly poured out on Howard, it was poisoning me in the process.

Slowly, like the layers of an onion, my wrong beliefs, my anger and my self protection were being painfully stripped away. I could see for myself that my behavior was underwritten with my own sinful strategies. My attention had been taken off what I perceived as Howard's deficiencies, and the spotlight was now shining with glaring intensity on what was in my heart.

No wonder the Bible gives these strong words of admonition in Proverbs: "Pay attention to what I say; listen closely to my words. Do not let them out of your sight, keep them within your heart; for they are life to those who find them and health to a man's whole body" (Prov. 4:20-22).

No wonder Jesus said, "Man does not live on bread alone, but on every word that comes from the mouth of God" (Matt. 4:4).

## *Intensive Care*

My eyes—and my heart—were being opened to a staggering reality: The Bible is not an inspired book of how-to's for errant children. It is a love letter about relationships—God's with us, and ours with God and others.

I had come to see that my whole self-protective approach to life was affecting my relationships with virtually everyone. And my wrong beliefs were never more clearly exposed than in my relationship with Howard. My whole approach to life and to marriage was 180 degrees from God's plan!

Mine was a self-serving, unloving and unscriptural approach. At the core, I had come into this marriage to get, not to give. Yes, change was needed; I was right about that. But the only person I could change was me.

This could be no mere outward adjustment either. I was embarking on a journey to discover what real love is. Up to this point in my life, I'd taken some wrong roads, but they had only sidetracked me. The truth is, there are no shortcuts or detours with God.

When you have walked according to wrong beliefs as long as I had, you don't change overnight. It takes time to learn a new way. In the ensuing days and weeks, the Spirit of truth continued to expose the attitudes in my heart. It was a veritable "stripping down" of my old beliefs as I weighed them against God's Word.

In his letter to the church in Ephesus, Paul writes about putting off "the old self" and putting on "the new." The passage speaks of growth in a graphic way:

> You were taught, with regard to your former way of life, to put off your old self, which is being corrupted by its deceitful desires...and to put on the new self, created to be like God in true righteousness and holiness (Eph. 4:22,24).

Paul picks up the same idea of taking off the old and putting on the new in his letter to the Colossians. (See Col. 3:9,10.) In both instances, the Greek words for taking off mean "disrobing," as in taking off an old coat.

Initially, I had come to Dick and Marilyn for help because my "old coat" was no longer adequate, and I thought I'd walk away wearing a "new coat."

But I was discovering that I needed more than a simple wardrobe change. I needed the Holy Spirit and the Word of God to radically realign my heart beliefs. In addition, I needed God's empowering grace to enable me to keep putting "on the new."

Radical? Yes.

But God's antidote for sin is nothing short of radical. His truth would not only be His instrument of healing, it would be my constant companion on the journey to love.

# $\mathscr{T}$HIRSTY $\mathscr{P}$ILGRIMS

The relentless rays of the midday sun beat down across my shoulders. I dug into my purse for dark glasses and another squeeze of suntan lotion to smooth over my arms and dab across my forehead. All morning I'd looked forward to this stop on our Holy Land tour: Jacob's Well, one of the most authenticated sites in all of Israel.

On this particular day, I was taking a break from a conference in Jerusalem, joining a group touring the high points of biblical history. I was relishing every minute of it! From the blustery boat ride across the Sea of Galilee between Tiberias and Capernaum, to the solemn sharing of the Lord's Supper at the Garden Tomb, I was falling in love with this little country.

I was hungry to take it all in—the gentle, rolling hills, the peaceful green valleys, the dusty roads, the little towns and the teeming city of Jerusalem. My mind savored every historical tidbit the tour guide dished out as he painted word pictures of life in Bible times.

But while my mind was busily absorbing the facts, my heart was warming to this little country of rocky fields, olive groves, shrines and archaeological digs. More than just being the historical center of our Judeo-Christian heritage, this place pulsated with life! And I knew I wasn't the first to feel it.

God's life was here in some inexplicably deep dimension, transcending all of history and every culture, and throbbing with His passionate heartbeat for the world.

That afternoon, the temperature hovered around 85 degrees in the Samaritan town of Nablus. "Come on, everybody. I know it's hot, but you need to see this site up close." The tour guide herded his busload of wilted tourists out of the air-conditioned coach, across the street and over to the dirt courtyard inside the ruins of an unfinished Greek Orthodox church.

My footsteps sent puffs of dust ballooning into the air, some so high they tickled my dry throat into an immediate sneeze. "This is the only well in the area that has been in continual use since the days of the patriarchs." The eager tour guide couldn't wait to tell us more. I leaned forward to catch his words, but I sneezed once more and missed half of his second sentence.

I rummaged back into my purse, this time for my handkerchief. Too late to block another sneeze. I again heard only a portion of what our guide was saying. Something about this being the spot where Jesus met the Samaritan woman and asked her for a drink of water.

## *An Empty Jar and an Empty Heart*

Jesus. The Samaritan woman. My mind leapt backward to the familiar scene by Jacob's Well, described so clearly in John's Gospel:

> Jesus, tired as he was from the journey, sat down by the
> well. It was about the sixth hour. When a Samaritan woman
> came to draw water, Jesus said to her, "Will you give me a

drink?" (His disciples had gone into the town to buy food.)

The Samaritan woman said to him, "You are a Jew and I am a Samaritan woman. How can you ask me for a drink?" (For Jews do not associate with Samaritans.)

Jesus answered her, "If you knew the gift of God and who it is that asks you for a drink, you would have asked him and he would have given you living water" (John 4:6-10).

Even as I stood there in the hot sun mentally replaying the story, I was struck with the parallel between the woman with her water jar and myself. In 2,000 years, the issue here hadn't changed; it was still thirst.

How well I knew it as my own dry throat clamored for relief. "How about a drink from Jacob's Well?"

I thought he'd never ask! Our tour guide knelt down at the top of the well and turned the crank that would bring up the cool, refreshing water. One at a time, he dipped out mini-cupfuls to us, sun-baked tourists with parched throats. My turn couldn't come quickly enough. I was thirsty!

So was the Samaritan woman whom Jesus met at the well. Yet her need went far deeper than mere physical thirst, and Jesus knew it. Filled with His Father's compassion, He looked beyond her promiscuous lifestyle and saw her heart, dry and barren, and thirsting for love.

Here they were, just the two of them alone at the well. One skeptical, tentative woman, desperately needing answers for her life. And Jesus, full of grace and truth, with the answer. Gently, but directly, He extended His offer: living water to quench the thirst in her heart.

We know the rest of the story. The Samaritan woman naively interpreted Jesus' gift of living water in the contemporary language of the Jewish people. To them, living water meant running water.[1] She knew the water of Jacob's Well had only percolated from the subsoil; it didn't bubble up from a free-flowing stream.

Where would Jesus have access to running water? Was He saying that He was somehow greater than Jacob who had dug this well for his family and his cattle? His offer, she thought, bordered on blasphemy.

Her curiosity, however, overrode her skepticism. She reached out for what Jesus had to offer. "Sir, give me this water so that I won't get thirsty and have to keep coming here to draw water" (John 4:15).

Jesus drew their verbal byplay to a close and told the woman to call her husband to join them at the well. With that one directive, her lifestyle was exposed. Yet, strangely, she didn't turn and run. "'I have no husband,' she replied" (John 4:17).

Seeing her openness, Jesus moved on to confront her gently with the facts of her relationships; she had had a terrible marriage record, and she was not legitimately married to the man with whom she was currently living.

How could Jesus have known about her past? Or her present? Was He a prophet? Quickly she put two and two together and questioned Jesus, who directly identified Himself as the Messiah.

## She Had Value

The Messiah! This astounding disclosure brought everything into place for this thirsty woman—at last! Here was One who knew all about her, yet He fully accepted her. In His eyes, she had value—as a woman, as a Samaritan, even as a sinner. Perhaps for the first time, she experienced what she'd been searching for all her life: love and acceptance. Her response? She opened her heart.

No longer bound by shame or her status as an outcast, she rushed back into town, leaving her water jar sitting in the dust by the well! *The whole town must know about this Man who "told me everything I ever did"* (John 4:39).

John records her one-woman evangelism thrust simply. "Many of the Samaritans from that town believed in him because of the woman's testimony" (John 4:39). Doesn't that say something about the depth of human thirst, when this kind of news pushes past people's long-standing cultural antagonisms and sends them running toward the well with empty cups?

## Backhoes and Jackhammers at Work

My physical thirst had been wonderfully assuaged that hot November afternoon at Jacob's Well. I'd also been deeply moved at rethinking the story of Jesus' tender love toward the Samaritan woman. I had a lot more in common with this woman than wanting water. Sure our strategies differed, but we were both thirsty for the same thing—someone to love us. We just went about pursuing "thirst quenchers" in different ways. Foolish ways.

She sought for love and meaning in her life through her long string of relationships with men. I took a different tack. But in a way I was pursuing exactly what the woman at the well was after: security—the feeling of being loved—and significance, the sense of having value.

While my approach was more socially correct, it was, nevertheless, the same: self-relating. I wanted to get my needs for security and significance met from my perfect performance as a wife and homemaker and from another person—Howard.

When I returned from Israel and began counseling again with Dick and Marilyn Williamson, this was the exact place they brought me to in an early session. "Jane, you are trying to get your needs met in Howard."

We must have come back to this statement a dozen or more times before there was even a crack of light in my understanding. My boiling anger was the tip-off. I was angry because all my attempts and strategies to get my needs met had failed.

"Change will come," Marilyn encouraged, "but it will take time to look at some of the heart beliefs you've held. Particularly the one that says you can get your needs met apart from God. That's the tough one, the core belief of what the Bible calls 'foolishness.'"

These counseling sessions with Marilyn and Dick comprised, without a doubt, some of the most productive, life-giving hours of my entire life. I was meeting with two people whose demeanor and patience exuded Jesus' love and caring and who were dedicated to helping me take responsibility for my reaction to the hurts of the past. They wanted to see me set free to love, even in the midst of pain. At the time, however, the sessions were often hard. At other times, glorious breakthroughs brought me to new ground.

To begin with, as my beliefs were hammered down by the clear teaching of the Word of God, I encountered emotional pain such as I'd never known. My way of thinking about life, about myself, about my marriage, even about God was challenged on every front. I've equated the process to heart surgery, but there were times when it also felt more like a gigantic remodeling project with backhoes and jackhammers having free reign in every corner of my life—with me in the middle cowering without a hard hat!

My thoughts and feelings took the full force of the construction project under way—sometimes bruised and battered, other times pushed to the joy of new freedom. My emotions had no choice but to roll with the program. I'd sit down at the kitchen table to read the Bible and journal in my notebook. I would write a few words, then break into tears over the pain of my self-centered approach, the way I'd lied to myself or my lack of love toward Howard. Sometimes I'd veer off course by justifying my actions, but then I'd flinch at my obvious self-righteousness.

At other times, I spewed out anger as my long-stuffed feelings of resentment gushed to the surface, surprising even me with their intensity. Through it all, Scripture became my plumb line; I recounted what had been said to me and then systematically dove into the Bible to clarify what I was hearing from God's Word. While it was all progress, I confess that many days I was certain I was riding a fast train backwards: destination death, not life.

Bit by bit, however, truth was penetrating my heart. The truth of God's Word was getting through, as well as the truth the Holy Spirit was unfolding to me personally, particularly on the issue of foolishness.

## Uncovering Foolishness

"When we try to get our needs for security and significance met apart from God, we always go to foolishness."

Dick's statement seemed clear, yet I couldn't fathom what he really meant. *Go to foolishness?* This phrase had no more meaning to me than "go to Chicago or New York." But the Williamsons followed up their statements with Scripture, verses I'd often read before but never grasped at a life-changing level.

At the close of one session, Dick and Marilyn said their good-byes and then Dick smiled and reminded me to meditate on Proverbs 22:15: "Foolishness is bound in the heart of a child" (*KJV*).

This particular proverb led me to a totally new understanding, not only of my role in our marriage, but my entire approach to life!

Foolishness. We are born with it. That's basically what "bound in the heart of a child" means. Our sin nature is bent on going *our* way, not God's. The word "bound" means "under compulsion." It is the inclination of our hearts. It may sound strong, but the truth is, we—every one of us—are born determined to go our own way.

And what is this foolishness that rules us? In his basic seminar, Dr. Larry Crabb defines it as "a conviction that life can be found apart from God." In his book *Inside Out* he goes on to say, "We long for a life that is real, full and happy. We think we can make this kind of life happen, so we take things into our own hands to try to make it take place."[2]

The inevitable fallout of this human-centered, self-directed, foolish life plan is that we develop into empty, lonely people. Our lives become disordered and racked with anxiety. We have broken marriages and sickness because our ways don't satisfy those needs of ours that are designed to be filled by our Creator. As we know, this development is nothing new; the history of God's covenant people is riddled with stories of their stubborn determination to go their own way and how God faithfully— and repeatedly—sent His messengers to call them back to Him. Listen, for instance, to the prophet Isaiah as he echoes this familiar cry of God's heart toward His people:

> This is what the Lord says—your Redeemer, the Holy One of Israel: "I am the Lord your God, who teaches you what is best for you, who directs you in the way you should go. If only you had paid attention to My commands, your peace would have been like a river, your righteousness like the waves of the sea" (48:17,18).

We don't have to look far to see evidence of this same destructive path all around us. Sadly, even among people who adamantly declare that their life and joy are found in the Lord Jesus, we see behavior that shows they really don't believe this in their hearts. There's a big gap between their confession and their reality.

Ever since man swallowed Satan's first lie in the Garden of Eden, we have been easily seduced away from godly thinking. Look for a moment at some of the foolish ideas we buy into, substituting the world's wisdom for God's wisdom.

- Money makes a man important.
- Living in the right house or neighborhood will establish me as an important person.
- If my husband loved me in the way I need and want, I would be fulfilled and happy as a woman.
- If I could find the right mate, I would be complete.
- If I could earn a college degree, I'd feel important among my peers.

- If I could attain the right weight, I'd feel attractive and acceptable as a woman.
- If I had enough money in the bank, I'd be secure.

Sounds like a contemporary list, doesn't it? However, the prophet Jeremiah might well have taken the same inventory in his day as he proclaimed God's Word to the Israelites: "My people have committed two sins: They have forsaken me, the spring of living water, and have dug their own cisterns, broken cisterns that cannot hold water" (Jer. 2:13). The driving human thirst for security and significance is timeless—as are the foolish beliefs that propel us to meet these needs apart from God, through our own strategies.

Although both men and women have these basic God-given needs, a man's stronger need is for significance, a woman's for security. Yet both set goals that they feel must be accomplished in order to have these needs met.

A man measures his significance by his position in life, his success on the job or the amount of money he earns. A woman, looking for security, turns to others, to her home, her career or her appearance to meet her needs.

## A Painful Illustration

One particular event that took place when Howard and I were first married illustrates my foolish attempts to gain acceptance through my outward appearance.

Howard and I had flown to Hawaii for a travel convention. One night we were to attend a special dinner party, one of those social "command performances" where there is no alternative but to "be there."

On a limited budget, I wore a simple dress I'd made and to which I'd added a few matching accessories, thinking I'd be comfortably appropriate for the evening.

I was completely unprepared for the bucket of insecurity that splashed over me as I walked in the door of the hotel's sumptuous dining room. My first thought was that we'd stumbled into the wrong room, that, by mistake, we'd walked into the governor's inaugural ball. The sight of dozens of elegantly dressed people nearly took my breath away!

The women looked like they had come straight out of the pages of *Vogue*. I saw one wearing an iridescent blue silk sheath, and another woman in a shimmering white sequin suit. They were all expensively dressed—designer clothes with complimentary jewelry. Their hair was perfectly coifed. Even their perfume filled the room with exclusive scents. I felt like Cinderella after midnight, standing at an exquisite ball dressed in her Simplicity Pattern #4682. I wanted to crawl back home, curl up in my jeans and eat a TV dinner.

Instead, I grabbed for my lifeline, Howard. He took my hand, introduced me to some of his coworkers, got me a glass of Coke, then left me with one of the wives as he moved across the room to talk and laugh with his friends in the travel business.

"Is this your first time in Hawaii?" Val, a lovely fortyish woman in a soft beige angora sweater and matching silk dress, twirled the straw in her ice tea and looked up at me with a pleasant smile.

But my mouth went dry, as if it were filled with cotton candy. I took a long sip of my Coke before I could even answer. "Well, yes, this is my first time here. Howard's been before." *That sounds so dumb, Jane. Can't you think of anything more exciting to talk about?*

But I couldn't. And the animated conversation going on around me only reinforced my negative self-critique. I couldn't think of what to say, how to act or what to do, except for one thing: feel hurt and angry at Howard. Why wasn't he standing by my side, giving me the moral support and confidence I needed to survive this awkward social situation?

*Adam &*
*Eve*

## The Blame Game

Blaming someone else. The reaction comes automatically when pain strikes us. Yet blame is only a smoke screen covering the insecurity in one's heart. Howard wasn't the problem; I was. My own sense of inferiority kept nipping at my heels like a persistent puppy. At that moment, under the dazzling chandeliers and standing by the exotic hors d'oeuvres table, I felt as though the whole room were shouting, "See Jane, you don't measure up!" In reality, however, the room was mute; the negative message I heard came from inside me.

As I looked toward Howard, I could feel anger and demandingness rise in me—a perfect illustration of the progression foolishness takes. First we have a wrong belief that others will meet our needs, then, gradually, a demand that they must meet them. When they don't, anger and resentment jump on the bandwagon and a full-scale parade marches destructively through our hearts.

How grateful I am that some thirty years after this dinner party, God rained on that little parade. He rained love and hope and forgiveness. And even more: He Himself came to march through my heart. Where I'd looked to people, things and appearances to fill up the emptiness I felt inside, where I'd projected an image that I thought would bring me acceptance and love, God came with the quiet, but certain truth that I was acceptable just as I was.

## It's Okay to Be Thirsty

Dr. Larry Crabb describes our plight as thirsty pilgrims: "We long for both respect and involvement, impact and relationship. In the desert of a fallen world, our soul is parched."[3] He goes on to say, "Every fallen person created to enjoy God is thirsty."[4]

Stop right there; that's the catch! We are thirsty for what we were created for—relationships. First with God, the One whose image we bear, and then with those around us. Wanting love and needing love are part of our makeup, our humanness.

GOD MADE US FOR RELATIONSHIP—
TO THIRST FOR HIM AND TO BE RICHLY
NOURISHED BY THE LOVE OF OTHERS.
WE NEED GOD AS WE NEED THE
VERY AIR WE BREATHE.

Why does God tell us over and over in the Scriptures that He loves us? Why does He command us to love Him and others? (See Matt. 22:37-39.) Why?

Because He made us that way.

He made us for relationship—to thirst for Him and to be richly nourished by the love of others. We need Him as we need the very air we breathe.

This side of heaven, we're all thirsty people longing for the security and significance we lost at the Fall. And it's okay to be thirsty. Jesus never chastised the Samaritan woman for having legitimate longings. Neither was there anything wrong with my longing to be loved. The problem lies in what we do to assuage our thirst—our self-centered strategies, our self-protection and lack of godly love.

My friend Connie tells what she did with the thirst in her heart. She denied it even existed. Coming from a broken home as a little girl of seven to live with an older aunt and uncle, she survived emotionally by becoming a high achiever and a people pleaser. Her strategy worked well into adulthood, until a few years ago when a problem cropped up in her family.

She made an appointment to talk with a pastor about the situation. Almost immediately the adept pastor sensed where he could really help Connie. He asked her if she felt her aunt and uncle loved her. Without thinking, she responded, "They did the best they could, but they were farmers, busy people."

The pastor faced her directly, "Don't you believe little girls need love?" She couldn't answer. He pressed her further, "I'd like you to say, 'I am a person who needs love.'" Such a simple request, but the words stuck in her throat as she tried to say them.

"I felt humiliated and horribly uncomfortable," she remembers. "It was all I could do to repeat the words, but I said them: 'I am a person who needs love.'"

For years, Connie had denied her God-given thirst for love. Her lack was too painful to look at. If she faced it, there was the very real possibility in her mind that she just might be unlovable. Without feeling loved, she had only one alternative—to live her life believing she didn't need any. So she did. She lived a "nice" life—distancing herself emotionally behind a self-protective wall.

Unfortunately, the lie she believed soon gave birth to another: that she was not acceptable as she was. An emotionally deprived child, she then set about vigorously meeting her needs on her own terms.

In her case, she pushed herself to achieve academically; from childhood through college, she drove herself to be first in every competition that came along. After all, there were always rewards to allay her sense of lack. Gold stars, applause, certificates, blue ribbons—these pathetic trophies became substitutes for the love she really wanted.

If Connie had somehow been present at the Feast of Tabernacles when Jesus taught at the temple courts, she would have known it was okay to be thirsty. Do you remember that wonderful scene on the last day of the Feast? In our day, we'd say Jesus was in hot water; the pressure was on among the chief priests and Pharisees to silence this rabble-rouser—once and for all.

Jesus, however, would not be silenced. He stood up and in a loud voice said, "If anyone is thirsty, let him come to me and drink" (John 7:37). He didn't say, "If you're thirsty, ignore it, deny it, stuff your feelings, compensate in some other way." No, He said, "If you're thirsty, COME!"

Jesus is still giving that same invitation today. It's okay to be thirsty. In fact, it's wonderful and blessed to be thirsty (see Matt. 5:6). But come, get water! Not just a cupful, but life-giving rivers of living water that will quench your thirst and flow out to others in eternal dimensions.

## An Appetite for Wisdom

When I was growing up, we often kidded about being members of the "clean plate club." My brother, Jimmy, and I were no exceptions to a common mealtime expectation of children in the '40s and '50s: "Eat whatever is put before you. If you don't like spinach or peas, you will when you get hungry enough."

My dad often took that illustration to the spiritual realm. He used to say, "If you go hungry long enough, you will gain an appetite for things of God you would not normally desire or seek after."

Looking back, I believe that this is precisely what God was allowing for me. He was wanting to show me what was in my heart—the foolish beliefs and empty pursuits that would not satisfy. It felt like a desert place, not unlike the wilderness He led His covenant people through.

You shall remember all the way which the Lord your God has led you in the wilderness these forty years, that He might humble you, testing you, to know what was in your heart, whether you would keep His commandments or not. And He humbled you and let you be hungry, and fed you with manna which you did not know, nor did your fathers know, that He might make you understand that man does not live by bread alone, but man lives by everything that proceeds out of the mouth of the Lord (Deut. 8:2,3, *NASB*).

In His love for us, the Lord allows our hunger and lack of satisfaction to intensify to a point where we begin to realize the emptiness of our barren pursuits. At the same time, our hearts and appetites are being awakened for God; He is the only One from whom we can draw life. Every other strategy is foolish. But where is the way out? What will turn us around?

There is only one thing: living our lives by godly wisdom. This is the direct opposite of living by human wisdom, which is foolishness before God.

"Get wisdom, get understanding; do not forget my words or swerve from them" (Prov. 4:5). Like manna in the wilderness, God's Word would feed my malnourished understanding and turn me from my man-centered orientation. Oh, how I needed that Word which would be "a lamp to my feet and a light for my path" (Ps. 119:105). Scripture after scripture began pointing me to the unequivocal wisdom of God and the absolute necessity of living by it.

"The fear of the Lord is the beginning of knowledge, but fools despise wisdom and discipline" (Prov. 1:7). Whether it is the collapse of a house foolishly built on sand (see Luke 6:49) or fools eating "the fruit of their ways" (Prov. 1:31), there are consequences when one chooses not to live by God's Word. And conversely there are benefits when one does: a house that stands when the storms hit (see Luke 6:48) and being safe "from the ways of wicked men" (Prov. 2:12).

I'd had enough of foolishness, the junk food of life.

I was tired of going my own way. I was hungry to be nourished with the bread and meat of wisdom and thirsty for the water that would satisfy.

## Changing Beliefs

Do you know what it feels like to begin a physical fitness regimen? To cut back on the fat grams and empty calories and plunge ahead with a vigorous exercise program? To me it spells "long haul, upward road, sweat and tears." Results won't come overnight. And it will take effort.

I felt that way often when Marilyn and Dick challenged my beliefs. I'd come to counseling to change Howard, and I'd been brought face-to-face with my need to change, not my husband, but myself. Knowing the truth, however, is always the beginning point of freedom. From that place, I could move toward the remedy which would bring the wholeness I needed so desperately.

Changing false beliefs is a path without shortcuts, a process of beginning to line up our lives with the Word of God. It is absolutely essential.

If your beliefs are incorrect, your whole life will be built on a wrong foundation. The apostle Paul knew what he was talking about when he said the way to be transformed is by "the renewing of your mind" (Rom. 12:2).

Let me summarize some practical, biblical steps I learned in this process of changing my wrong beliefs:

1. Admit what you believe in your heart.
   - When there are recurring negative feelings, find the unbiblical pattern you are following. There is a root problem you need to identify.
   - Deal with the root problem rather than rehashing the same old feelings and issues. God wants

us to be reconciled and to let go of the lie once
and for all.

2. Confess what you believe. (To yourself, to the Lord, to
   others.)

3. Repent of your belief. (Compare your belief with the
   Scriptures. How does it compare with godly beliefs?)
   - Repent for coming against God's Word. Many
     people weep over their pain, but not their sin.
     Repentance is essential. From the Greek word
     *metanoia*, repentance means to turn around and
     go another direction.
   - Own your action as sin against God.
   - Make a deliberate decision to turn from it.

4. Ask the Lord's forgiveness. "Lord, I am totally wrong.
   Please forgive me for putting my truth before the Truth."

5. Receive His forgiveness. The biggest problem many of
   us face is allowing ourselves to be forgiven. We feel we
   must be punished or pay.
   - Choose to receive God's love and cleansing and
     forgive yourself.

6. Walk in the new belief. (Line up your beliefs with the
   Word of God. "I am totally wrong; Lord, you are total-
   ly right.")
   - Let the Word of God continue to be the basis for
     your new belief.

There will be many tendrils attached to the roots of our false
beliefs. We will see the harm our false—or ungodly—beliefs have
done to us. As this happens, ask the Lord to totally forgive you
for that false belief that has harmed you so. And He will.

Walking in God's truth is much like planting a garden. Seed
will go into the ground. It will need to be watered while you wait
for it to grow. God's Word will not return empty (see Isa. 55:11),
and the Holy Spirit will be there to bring it to life.

## Come and Drink

True, I'd been a stumbling, thirsty pilgrim looking for life in all the wrong places, believing the wrong things. But the same Jesus who met the Samaritan woman at the well also had water for my parched soul. From the barren wilderness of Palestine before Christ, from the hot sands of Egypt, from the dusty villages of Jesus' day, to the bleak, hopeless desert places of our lives, God still offers life-giving water to thirsty pilgrims.

"Come, all you who are thirsty, come to the waters; and you who have no money, come..." (Isa. 55:1).

# OUT OF HIDING

I did not learn to walk in the fullness of God's truth overnight. Instead, it was a process of replacing my wrong beliefs one by one, then taking my first steps like a child learning to walk. God, in His wonderfully creative way, used other people and a variety of situations to teach me.

One of these learning moments took place during a casual lunch with friends. Bill, his wife, Marilyn, Howard and I were laughing and chatting together over seafood salads when I made an insignificant remark. Bill cocked his head and chuckled before he spoke. "Jane, you're like a private country club."

I put down my glass of water and did a double take. A private country club? These words came from a man whose opinion I respected and who, I felt, knew me well. Howard and I had spent time together with Bill and Marilyn.

"Bill, what on earth do you mean?" I asked.

He smiled, and answered in a gently teasing tone, "Only a few get in, Jane."

His observation jolted me. Was I some kind of a snob? I loved people; surely he couldn't accuse me of being exclusive.

Funny, isn't it, how we view ourselves? I never thought of myself as being a "closed" person. Reserved, quiet—that's how I would have described my personality. Being the life of the party was outside my comfort zone, but I saw myself as warm and friendly.

Yet I couldn't ignore Bill's comment. Was he saying I was a closed person?

Immediately, I had a mental picture of a palatial clubhouse, fronted by massive white pillars, surrounded by acres of perfectly edged lawn. Flowers were everywhere, set in nursery-perfect rows. It was the kind of private club you see in movies where you drive down a long, narrow road blocked by an imposing gate. When you stop, you have to pass a litmus test to prove you belong. The comparison unsettled me.

## *Facing the Issue of Openness*

The country club issue didn't go away.

Sometime later in a counseling session, Dick and Marilyn asked me to share something of my childhood with them. When I got to the crisis in my parents' marriage during those traumatic days in Glendale, Dick stopped me. "We need to look at how you reacted here, Jane. You were afraid, a little girl feeling like her world was falling apart in front of her, and, of course, you had a reaction."

Dick paused for a moment to search my face before he continued. Then, soberly and directly, he said, "When you vowed that no man would ever hurt you like your father hurt your mother, you closed emotionally."

*Closed? That word again.* I looked across the table, puzzled. *Do people open and close like swinging doors?* The concept was still new to me. But from then on, we began dealing with other points in my childhood that had also contributed to many decisions that I had made to close my heart to others.

Still, even at this stage, I wondered why Dick and Marilyn were making such an issue about openness. What was wrong with being reserved, with not speaking your mind every time? It seemed to me that complete openness was a goal of questionable worth that might hold more trauma than deliverance.

When I took this issue before the Lord, however, He showed me in Scripture where openness was always in His plan and why it was vital to my healing.

## God's Perfect Plan

From the beginning, God had a plan. He would have a family, a people, a race, a nation through whom He would reveal Himself. As the doors of time open, we hear these words: "Let us make man in our image, in our likeness" (Gen. 1:26).

The Hebrew word for "image," according to *Strong's Concordance*, means "representative figure." Think about this in terms of the story of Adam and Eve, whom we meet in the Garden of Eden, the very ones God created who would walk in relationship with Him and represent Him on earth. Adam and Eve (and all who followed them) would be the family God wanted, the people who would express His life in the world. One of the ways they would do this would be through the vehicle of relationship.

## Paradise Lost

In God's garden paradise, Adam enjoyed unclouded fellowship with his Creator. Complete openness. No tension. No distancing. No walls to stop the natural flow of love and fellowship between them.

No walls, that is, until sin entered with its terrible consequences. Consequences so wrenchingly tragic, they affected all the created order. At the time of the Fall, man became separated from God, from those around him, even from himself.

Adam not only ran to hide, he tried to cover himself as well. But his Creator/Father was fast on his heels, His tender cry resounding across paradise, "Where are you?" (Gen. 3:9).

Adam's incredibly revealing answer followed, "I heard you in the garden, and I was afraid because I was naked; so I hid" (Gen. 3:10). Fear propels us to self-protection.

Ashamed of his nakedness, stricken by his failure, fearing exposure, Adam turned away from God. Hiding was the only escape he knew. Fearing rejection, he covered his body with fig leaves and his heart with a shield of fear. What he was created for—fellowship with God and others—was broken.

Man closed his heart.

There are no words to fully express—or even define—the impact this choice had on humankind. Closedness is first motivated by fear, shame and hurt, and then when it happens, these same emotions become deeply internalized, suffocating God-given life in the human heart.

Pastor and author Dr. A.W. Tozer wrote about these issues:

> Hardly anything reveals so well the fear and uncertainty among men as the length to which they will go to hide their true selves from each other and even from their own eyes. Almost all men live from childhood to death behind a semi-opaque curtain, coming out briefly only when forced by some emotional shock and then retreating as quickly as possible into hiding again. The result of this life-long dissimulation is that people rarely know their neighbors for what they really are, and worse than that, the camouflage is so successful that they do not know themselves either.[1]

## Satan's Attack on God's Plan

Even before Adam's sin, God's plan was brutally attacked. Lucifer (Satan) rose up against God. He rebelled against the Ruler of the Universe, wanting to exalt himself above the Most High God. He wanted two things: preeminence (the opposite of humility) and independence (the opposite of dependence, which is an ingredient of relationship with God and others). In his craving to be first, Satan struck a blow at relationships because he knew it was through relationships that God would reveal Himself in the earth.

Since the time of the Fall, we, too, have sought those two qualities: preeminence and independence. We want preeminence in relationships. We also seek to maintain independence and self-protection rather than interdependence and the giving of ourselves. These acts of our will counter the very purpose God has for relationships.

Remember, God's plan is that His people would reveal His life in the earth. Relationships are the key to demonstrating His nature. The reason Satan attacks relationships is to destroy the image of God in the earth. If the enemy can cause us to falter in the area of relationships, if he can cause us to close our hearts to one another, he succeeds in defaming the image of God, and we are left with no testimony.

Satan continues to this day to wreak havoc in our hearts with his press for preeminence and independence. His old refrain has never varied: Be independent of God; seek life on your own terms.

## God's Relationship Basics

Jesus is emphatic on this issue of relationship as it affects unity among believers. We hear it clearly in His high priestly prayer:

> My prayer is not for them alone. I pray also for those who will believe in me through their message, that all of them may be one, Father, just as you are in me and I am in you (John 17:20).

It is not unity for the sake of cozy togetherness; it is unity with an eternal purpose. Jesus prayed, "May they be brought to complete unity to let the world know that you sent me and have loved them even as you have loved me" (John 17:23).

Clearly, the whole gospel is built on relationships, open relationships. Everything we do in our Christian walk is built on relationship with God and then with others. Let me enumerate:

- We begin our life in Christ with a relationship. This covenant relationship with Jesus is foundation for all other relationships.
- The Ten Commandments deal with relationships. The first four cover relationship with God, the last six with one another.
- Marriage is to be lived out in the context of relationship, with true commitment, true companionship and true communion.
- Parenting is built on relationship.
- The Body of Christ is relational in nature.

Edith Schaeffer, interviewed in *Focus on the Family* magazine, speaks to the crucial issue of relationships in families. "There is hard work to be done in relationships. Fifty years of love and appreciation do not come in a package with the marriage vows."[2]

It is imperative that families understand how openness needs to enter into the flawed, human parts of their relationships. Schaeffer suggests that a mother explain to her children, "I'm not perfect, your dad isn't perfect, none of us is perfect. We're just a lot of imperfect people living under the same roof for just a limited number of years." But, she says, the reward of continuity in family life is worth the work.[3]

Her description is a beautiful picture of the family of God, the Body of Christ, as it is on earth: I'm not perfect, you're not perfect, none of us is perfect. We're a lot of imperfect people living under one covering. But God, in His infinite wisdom, knew that the plan of having a family in the earth would best fulfill His purpose—for Himself, for humankind and, ultimately, in the countering of Satan's rule in this age called Time.

The Church (God's family) is made up of people who are not whole because of Adam's sin and our subsequent choices. Jesus Himself made this quite clear: "It is not the healthy who need a doctor, but the sick....I have not come to call the righteous, but sinners" (Matt. 9:12,13).

We need to remember that we came to Jesus all undone, not all put together. We came in need of a Savior/Physician. The Church, in one sense of the word, is a hospital, a place where the imperfect, the hurting, the wounded—those in need of restoration—come to be loved, accepted, encouraged and helped toward wholeness. This will only happen as we are healed in the area of our relationships. And our first step in this direction is learning to be open people.

## The Anatomy of Openness

How do we get back to the openness man experienced before the Fall? What steps can we take?

My adventure toward openness started with a decision I made at my kitchen table. When I finally saw how all my relationships were stalemated at a surface level, I chose to open up my heart. That's the first step: making a choice to be open.

*Webster's Dictionary* defines openness as "a state which permits unobstructed entrance or exit. Not closed, not covered, clogged or shut. A state which permits freedom of view. Not enclosed, fenced in, sheltered or covered over. A lack of pretense. Expanded, as an open book."

Openness is:

- More of an attitude than an action.
- A feeling we give other people that we are willing to share our hearts, our real selves down inside, without fear.
- A willingness to be known.

- A willingness to risk disclosing ourselves, which always brings with it the risk of being misunderstood, criticized, hurt, rejected or judged. But because we are growing in our capacity to trust God and His love for us, we are willing to entrust ourselves to one another.

Honesty and truthfulness are critical in our pursuit of God. The psalmist asks how we may be near God: "Lord, who may dwell in your sanctuary? Who may live on your holy hill?" (Ps. 15:1).

The answer: "He who walks uprightly, and works righteousness, and speaks the truth in his heart" (Ps. 15:2, *NKJV*).

The real key to both relationship with God and with others is that it is necessary to speak truth in our own hearts—to be honest with ourselves about ourselves.

When we are open and honest with God, our "closedness" that kept His love from being felt is removed. Love can flow in and love can flow out. Only then are we in a position to be open on the horizontal level. Our hearts are protected by God's love so we can risk being open to those around us. Love now has a chance.

## Hiding Is Closing

Let's take a look at the other side of the issue.

Hiding emotionally is like the child's game of hide-and-seek. You dart out of sight, find a secret place, and when someone comes looking for you, you remain breathlessly still, out of their sight. Your goal is to stay so well hidden, you are never seen or caught.

Like Adam, I tried to conceal my imperfections in hopes that I could keep the real truth about me from others. I lived with a pervasive sense of unacceptability to others and judgments against myself. Not only did I hide the "real Jane," I presented the world with another Jane, one of my own making and one I'd gotten quite comfortable with.

Pastor David Seamands, in his book *Healing for Damaged*

*Emotions*, aptly describes this same path I took—from hiddenness to projecting an image:

> Somewhere in the process of growing up, the child receives messages about himself, about God, about people and about relationships. These messages can be taught or caught. They can come through what is directly said or done, or what is not said or not done....The child who has received negative messages then knows: "I am not accepted and loved as I am. I've tried every way to get this approval by being the way I am. Now I can only be accepted and loved if I become something else and someone else."[4]

## Pseudo Jane

Dick and Marilyn lovingly helped me to identify this pseudo Jane. I'd learned at an early age that people can be critical, judgmental and hurtful. As a sensitive child who perceived she was unacceptable, I could not risk being vulnerable to people. That risk terrified me. In order to survive, I felt I had to make myself acceptable, to carve out another Jane to present to the world.

Dr. Seamands goes on to shed light on this familiar human process:

> The youngster doesn't sit down and figure this all out....Some very necessary feelings never come across to him, feelings like security, acceptance, belongingness and value. His need to be loved and to learn to give love is not met. Instead there develops a growing deep anxiety and feelings of insecurity, unworthiness and undesirableness. And the youngster begins to climb the long, torturous trail of trying to become someone else.[5]

How subtle, yet how grievous the transition is from what Dr. Seamands calls the "real you" to the "super you." According to him, "The super you is a false, idealized image you think you have to be in order to be loved and accepted."[6]

My "super you" translated to "superwoman." I didn't fly through the air in blue tights and a cape or soar over skyscrapers, but I did fly around inside myself in my attempt to be perfect. I was the one who had to do it right, say it right, look right—and never smudge my mascara.

My false strategy was brought to light and challenged as I sat at Dick and Marilyn's table.

Dick posed a hard question to me. "Jane, what if everything that surrounds you was stripped away from you—husband, children, your home, your possessions, your position, ministry, finances?" he asked. "What if it were all gone? What would be left? Who is the real person inside? Do you believe that these are the things that make you acceptable?"

What do you say to a challenge that specific? It was sobering. I who hated phoniness was seeing that, in my desire to be acceptable, I had without knowing it become less than real. Part of me wanted to run for the nearest fig leaf outlet store.

## Graven Images

After our counseling session, I drove home, jarred by the directness of Dick's question. At the same time, I was motivated to discover my honest answer.

The miles sped by while I considered what I'd just learned. Meanwhile, I subconsciously noted the billboards, the little tugs plying up Union Slough off Puget Sound, the pulp mill chimneys of Everett puffing out white smoke—all the sights I had come to know so well along this route.

Into this emotional and geographical potpourri, the Holy Spirit dropped two little words: graven image. I chuckled aloud. *What a God! He doesn't waste any time; He talks to His kids right in the middle of a busy freeway.*

I found the reference right away that evening after dinner, hunched over the kitchen table with my Bible, my dictionary and my coffee. "Thou shalt not make thee any graven image" (Deut. 5:8, *KJV*).

Graven image. The dictionary brought clarity. "Graven" means something carved out or sculpted. "Image" means an imitation or representation. The golden calf the Israelites made in Moses' absence is a good illustration: a lifeless, powerless, man-made object of worship. God's Word is inalterably clear on graven images. However, I'd always viewed this commandment solely in the context of pagans in unchristianized lands.

Now this passage was speaking to me with a contemporary— and personal—ring.

God wanted me to put away my idea of what a super mother should be, what a wife should be, a leader should be. I would have to pull down my image of what I thought others expected me to be.

Here again, Dr. Tozer's words underscore the crucial nature of the issue at stake:

> Self-knowledge is so critically important to us in our pursuit of God and His righteousness that we lie under heavy obligation to do immediately whatever is necessary to remove the disguise and permit our real selves to be known.[7]

Once more, my kitchen table became the scene of Kingdom business. I reread the scripture from Deuteronomy and confessed my sin of erecting a graven image—a false projection of myself. Now I could see it as a sin against the Lord and others. I repented for going my own way and made a decision to be an open person.

For the first time in my life, I was willing to be known for who and what I was.

*Idol = who/what we wish we were not what*

## The Real Jane

Change is rarely comfortable. In those next few weeks and months, I often felt out of control. I even feared that I would feel

*truth in its 1st light usually appears negative*

naked without my familiar cover-up. But I continued to fight years of ingrained habits and wrong reactions, and soon I made some extraordinary discoveries that gradually erased my fears.

People were responding to the real Jane. At work, people mentioned that my face looked less strained, that I seemed more at ease, more approachable. I'd hear, "What's happened to you, Jane?"

I couldn't always give a clear explanation except to say that God was at work. More than anything, I was aware of a growing love for those around me and a freedom to express that love.

## Beginning a Real Marriage Relationship

God was also at work in our home. As my guard came down, my self-protection being stripped away, I started sharing the real Jane with Howard. And he began to feel safe in our relationship in a way that allowed him to share the real Howard with me.

We started walking together in the mornings along the Edmonds waterfront, above the ferry landing, where we had a full view across Puget Sound to the rugged Olympic Mountains in the west. Somehow our pleasure doubled when we shared this awesome sight together.

Often on these walks, Howard and I talked about the ordinary, mundane things in our lives—when we should trade in our car or how we could update our kitchen. Sometimes we shared the deep secrets of our hearts, asking for forgiveness or praying for each other and our family. We prayed for Aglow, the nations and the current world situation.

We savored every moment, from the first step along the bluff above the water to our little finale in the Scandinavian bakery, where we had coffee and split a muffin before returning to our busy schedules.

Openness, we were discovering, was "the stuff" of our new relationship. It was so good just to be ourselves together amidst all the flurry of the harbor activity. Seagulls included.

And that's an irony worth noting. For here below the noisy, squabbling seagulls, our hearts, once so injured and distant, were

WHY ARE WE ALWAYS SURPRISED AT
THE TRUTH OF GOD'S WORD? IT PROVIDES
PRACTICAL DAY-TO-DAY, GUTSY-LIVING
REALITY—AND IT'S SIMPLE ENOUGH
TO UNDERSTAND!

discovering a new bond of love and peace. The squawk of the seagulls, after all, is no match for the song of lovebirds!

## God's Word Is True

Howard and I were so busy enjoying each other's company, we hardly noticed that a transition in our marriage was happening right under our noses. Intimacy and closeness, the feelings I'd struggled so hard to pound into our marriage, were being felt by both of us as a new, rich love flourished. God worked in our lives in ways I had never imagined.

Why are we always surprised at the truth of God's Word? It provides practical day-to-day, gutsy-living reality, and it's simple enough to understand.

## The Advocate of Openness

Jesus always advocated realness and openness. Look at the way He welcomed little children. He loved their vulnerability. "Let the little children come to me and do not hinder them, for the kingdom of heaven belongs to such as these" (Matt. 19:14).

He even went so far as to say that the childlike stance was a prerequisite for getting to God in the first place: "I tell you the truth, unless you change and become like little children, you will never enter the kingdom of heaven" (Matt. 18:3).

## Openness on Wheels

Let me share with you a recent experience with openness I witnessed in my own front yard.

One Saturday I'd gotten up early to attack the weeds sneaking in between our azaleas and rhododendrons. As I worked my way around the plants, I heard an unmistakable noise.

Looking up, I saw three little boys riding their bikes up our cul-de-sac for all they were worth. Their infectious laughter gave the weeds in front of me a reprieve as I stopped to watch the boisterous trio crisscrossing the street. Hilarity dressed in jeans. Adventure in high gear.

"Hey, guys, watch me!" The tallest boy pulled rank over his younger friends, pedaled like crazy and hung a wheelie that earned him their immediate respect.

"Wow!" the others chorused, stopping for a brief second before they pumped their way back up to the crest of the hill.

Suddenly, the littlest boy, pedaling behind them, screeched to a halt and yelled, "Hey, everybody, stop." As if under military orders, the others braked and turned around. When the little boy had their full attention, he addressed them with dead earnestness:

"Hey, you guys...do you like me?" The clear, poignant question filtered out across the street with all the immanence of a naked toddler streaking through the house after his bath. I put down my trowel and leaned forward.

The older boy looked at his young friend for a second and answered emphatically, "Sure we like you."

"Yeah, we like you," echoed the other boy. No hesitation. No snickers. No laughter.

Issue resolved. The contented boy mounted his bike again, and together they rode off to the crest of the hill.

"Do you like me?"

I thought about this question, posed without a shred of embarrassment, as I bagged up the weeds and carried them to the garbage can. The little boy asked outright what his heart honestly wanted to know. His openness gripped me.

When I mentioned it to Howard at dinner that evening, we began to speculate about a comparable adult scenario.

"Imagine a chief executive officer of an international corporation suddenly getting up from the boardroom table and addressing his directors, 'Excuse me, but I have to ask you a really important question....'" I began to laugh.

Howard, grinning, jumped in. "They'd put down their Mark Cross pens, stare at the man in his custom-tailored suit and wait expectantly for something profound."

We could see the whole scene unfold: The executive's question followed by awkward silence, nervous glances. Would any of those directors stand up and congratulate him for his honesty? Not on your life!

Because the world says it's not okay to open up your heart like that. It's weak. It's one thing for an eight-year-old boy in jeans and tennis shoes to be honest, but a grown man? The world tells him he's foolish.

## The Uncomfortable Question

You see, there's more here than an honest question. The reason the executive's question would make them so uncomfortable is because it would touch their own self-protection. It would finger the places where these men and women long ago had learned to hide the real person inside them. His transparency would make them feel embarrassed to admit their own need for love and acceptance.

Suppose, for instance, that genuine honesty spread through the boardroom after the question was posed. Suppose that the executive vice president stood up, cleared her throat and said, "Yes, I like you, and furthermore, I respect your honesty. But now I need to know something....Do you like me?"

Then maybe, just maybe, some brave soul would jump to his feet and confess, "There's a hole inside my heart so big, I feel it can never be filled up. But I've been afraid to tell you how empty I feel."

Most of us know only too well those same feelings, whether the setting is a corporate skyscraper, a church pew or at the family dinner table. How many times have we been part of a group or social gathering, aching on the inside but wearing a smiley mask on the outside?

The same mask that we think protects us also imprisons the knot of emptiness inside and prevents others from seeing our real selves. *"protection" —> bondage of prison*

## The Mask of Self-Protection

Protection has its positive aspects, too. God created us with a built-in security system. When we are threatened physically or emotionally, we instinctively react to protect ourselves from harm.

We have neither tortoise shell nor a skunk's offensive spray as a shield, but we do have inborn defense mechanisms to protect us against pain. Whether it is the surge of adrenaline that carries us through an accident or the blinking of an eye to wash away dust, we can be grateful to our Creator for this healthy aspect of self-protection.

However, it was the profoundly negative side aspect of our protective strategies that I had learned to see in myself.

I could never have skidded my bike to a stop and asked my

friends, "Hey, do you like me?" I couldn't risk being myself when that self didn't feel valued.

We protect ourselves in dozens of ways from being exposed or known and thus remain closed people. Here are just some of the major behaviors we use as protection:

- We use anger in two ways: to put people off and to stay away from our own pain.
- We use laughter to hide our real feelings and stay in surface relationships.
- We use talkativeness or quietness as a way of staying hidden.
- We use intellectualism, displayed by a superior attitude or lofty speech, to distance ourselves from others.
- We use flirting as surface behavior that puts off real relationship.
- We use a need to be right to cover the flawed real self inside.

By adulthood, I'd wrapped myself like a mummy in the shroud of my own self-protective strategies. But I was totally unaware that I'd moved to a dishonest lifestyle, closed to those around me and not giving them access to the real Jane. My mask was glued in place, projecting respectability and an "I've-got-it-all-together" image.

Perfectionism is self-oriented and self-gratifying. In short, it is worldly behavior.

Instead of becoming vulnerable sinners in need of God's grace and the cleansing power of Jesus' blood, we tend to become performance-oriented. But performance is not the ticket to Kingdom living. You can only get there on a train called the Grace and Mercy Express!

Here's the good news: For every detour sinful man takes, God offers a U-turn toward Kingdom living. He alone holds the map to bring us out of hiding and get us back on track to where the living is free, where love flows and relationship is rich and satisfying.

Let me tell you about one of those turnaround experiences I had when God's truth touched me—literally.

I attended the World Map Camp Meeting in Penticton, British Columbia, Canada. Following the meeting, Jack Hayford, senior pastor of Church On The Way in Van Nuys, California, looked at me and said, "I feel I need to pray for you before you leave."

He knelt beside my chair, praying quietly in the Spirit. "I feel that the Lord is telling me to peel a mask off of your face," he said to me. I felt him touch my cheek as he began the motion of peeling off a covering over my countenance. He began at the chin, then up over my cheeks, my eyes and finally over my forehead.

At the time, I knew something profound was happening. This man of God, under guidance from the Holy Spirit, foreshadowed perfectly what the Lord would do in me during the next few years.

The facade that covered my face was being peeled off in preparation for a new work of God.

## The Open-Hearted Church

Larry Crabb encourages believers to make a commitment to openness. He says, "The Church needs leaders who can involve themselves in other people's lives with the joy of integrity and transparency, confident that their love is unfeigned, willing to be deeply known for the sake of helping others."

But a word of caution: In this age of "anything goes," we need to approach openness with godly wisdom. Openness does not mean telling everybody everything at any time for no reason. Openness is not a license, it is an attitude of the heart.

Because it is an attitude of the heart—a feeling of openness that comes from within—there is an availability to my heart that was not there before, a willingness to share my heart out of a motive of love and commitment to helping others in their pursuit of God.

When we are more committed to becoming the person God created us to be, rather than protecting the person we have pretended to be, we will find our way out of hiding into openness—and more fully into the purpose of God. But that requires humble confession, repentance and a choice to seek God's face at every turn.

# *The* *Face*

# OF *Forgiveness*

If you've had kids, my guess is that you've also had mud tracked in on the living room carpet, a window broken from a stray baseball and perhaps a car fender dented when your novice driver made a solo run to the grocery store. As Edith Schaeffer said about families, "We're a lot of imperfect people living under the same roof."[1] Sometimes we rub more than just shoulders; we rub each other the wrong way.

Everyone expects a few rough spots when relating to people, whether it's in a family, in a job, at school or even at church. Maybe it's an upset over something as minor as missing a dental appointment or forgetting to take a phone message. Falling in the category of minor "bumps" on the road of life, these incidents are usually quickly dismissed with a casual, "Oh, you're forgiven. Forget it. It's okay."

What is harder to dismiss, however, is the aching sting of a deep, personal hurt that continues to generate inner turmoil. It has penetrated so deeply you wonder if you will be scarred forever. Sometimes the pain is so tangibly present, you're convinced it has lodged permanently in the lining of your heart, where, unknown to anyone but you, it silently bleeds your life away.

I can relate to that kind of pain. For years my personal diagnosis could well have been charted: "Undealt-with pain. Bruised. Tender. Internal bleeding."

Perhaps for you, it was a recent event when harsh words or a trusted friend's betrayal caught you unaware, delivering an unexpected blow from behind. It could have been that a family member verbally assaulted you or even sexually abused you. As a result you may feel deeply humiliated and devalued as a person. Or maybe you came from a "good" family. You lacked nothing materially but, at the same time, you never received the nurturing love and affirmation you needed as a child. Your empty heart yearned for love and acceptance and when you did not get it, you grew up with an emotional void inside. To this day you carry the ache of that deprivation.

In such situations our response is never as simple as, "Forget it. It's okay." This isn't like getting mud on the carpet. We can't just phone the rug cleaners in the morning and have them remove the pain by afternoon.

## A Picture of Pain

Let me tell you about my friend Julie. The youngest of twelve children, she was born into a poor but warm and loving Kentucky family. Her mother died when she was six months old, her father when she was two. For a time, her sisters struggled valiantly to keep the family together, but eventually Julie was placed in a foster home.

Not just one foster home, but a succession of them. Good, solid homes, most of them Christian, where Julie received loving care. Still, it wasn't the same as being in her own family, and Julie grew up feeling like an outsider, like she didn't really belong. Typical of children in similar situations, she found a way to compensate for her insecurity: she became a "good little girl," always on her best behavior for fear of being sent away—again.

Eager to learn, Julie did well in school and, wanting to be a teacher, enrolled in a Christian college. Here she met Ross, the son of missionaries, who was also studying to become a teacher. They shared the same values, the same faith, the same interests in art, history and travel. Not surprisingly, they fell in love and were married shortly after graduation.

The rest followed in storybook fashion: teaching jobs, a lovely first home, two wonderful little boys and opportunities to serve in their church, Ross as an elder and Julie as a Sunday School teacher. In addition, Julie led a Good News Club in her home, a Christian outreach for the neighborhood children.

Life was good for Julie. She had found the security she always wanted. It came wrapped up in a husband who loved her, two children to nurture and a home of her own.

Then without warning, her world caved in.

As he'd done every morning of their married life, Ross kissed Julie good-bye on his way out the door to school. However, when he returned home that evening, he did not kiss her. Instead, he walked into the kitchen, paced nervously for a few minutes, reached for a glass of water, swallowed a few mouthfuls and turned to face his wife. "I no longer love you, Julie," he blurted out. "I love my secretary. And I want a divorce."

Stunned that her husband of twenty years had been having an affair, and that he had chosen to leave his wife and family for another woman, Julie plunged into the deepest emotional turmoil of her life. As if pierced by a dagger, her heart beat with the wound of rejection and betrayal, even to the point of suicide.

Fear gripped her. How would she ever marshal enough strength to support her boys, 8 and 15, as they wrestled with the devastation in their lives? For Julie, this would not be one night's bad dream; the upheaval in her life would evolve into a ten-year nightmare.

More than once she felt like a rag doll that had been carelessly tossed to the side of the road. Left in a dust heap, no longer "special" to the one she'd entrusted her heart to. Dealing simultaneously with rejection, loneliness, lack of money and, eventually, both sons on drugs and alcohol, there were days when she feared her little home, once the safe harbor for a happy family and the gathering spot of the Good News Club, would never again be filled with joy and laughter.

To compound Julie's pain, Ross, now remarried and settled across town in a new condo, was busy boating, traveling—and ignoring his sons. His carefree, affluent lifestyle poured salt on Julie's open wounds.

## A Stain in the Heart

Can you imagine the bitterness that would enter in the wake of such devastation? Here was Julie, caught in a series of excruciating events she neither asked for nor had any control over. She was the innocent victim of another's self-centered choices.

Whatever the outside source, emotional pain like Julie's invariably lodges in the heart. Undealt with, it remains like a stubborn stain in the fabric of our lives, coloring everything we do with its sorrowful tinge. Even more destructively, it prompts us to close our hearts in self-protection, building walls— between us and God and between us and those around us.

Sadly, this kind of penetrating pain rarely goes away on its own. It doesn't don its hat one day, wave good-bye and walk away whistling down the street. No, unnoticed it burrows underground where it quietly fuels anger and resentment, then surfaces when something or someone else triggers it again. Neither innocent nor dormant, it has the potential of locking us in prisons of bitterness for years.

Just ask "Dear Abby." In response to one of her syndicated columns on forgiveness, she was deluged with letters describing how hatred and bitterness had robbed her readers of years of rich relationships.

One woman confessed, "I had an older brother who had given me genuine cause to hate him since I was 12 years old. I am now 75."

Another woman wrote, "I have spent at least 30 of my 42 years hating my mother."[2]

What help is there for dealing with this kind of pain—for the people locked in bitterness, for the Julies of this world, so wounded by unfair treatment? What help is there for victims of abuse? What recourse is there for those suffering painful childhood hurts, passed on from well-meaning parents who did not love in a way their children found fulfilling? Where is the way out of these painful prisons?

The Bible is clear: There is help for those incarcerated by such woundedness. Listen to Jesus' own words: "The Spirit of the Lord is on me, because he has anointed me to preach good news to the poor. He has sent me to proclaim freedom for the prisoners" (Luke 4:18). And again, in the Old Testament picture of the Messiah: "He has sent me to bind up the brokenhearted, to proclaim freedom for the captives" (Isa. 61:1). Jesus Himself is the help. Yes, He holds in His hands the key that will unlock the doors of our emotional prisons. And He has paid dearly for it.

Look closely at His nail-scarred hands. Do you see the key? It's stamped there: Forgiveness.

Jesus identifies with our pain. He Himself wept over Jerusalem, and He wept at the death of His friend Lazarus. We know He hurt. He was "a man of sorrows, and acquainted with grief" (Isa. 53:3, KJV). And He knows we hurt. "For we do not have a high priest who is unable to sympathize with our weaknesses" (Heb. 4:15).

Here He is, the Son of Man, relating to our frailty. His Father-heart cannot bear to leave us closed and locked behind bars of self-protection when we fail to deal with the hurts in our lives. Too wounded to receive His redemptive love, we stand empty-handed, with nothing to share with others. However, God is present in our pain, loving and accepting us, and wanting to rescue us from its trap.

Satan, however, prefers to keep us ensnared, and he tempts us at this very point to stay in our bitterness.

*Strong's Concordance* defines temptation as "an enticement to sin." That's precisely Satan's strategy when it comes to our hurts, our resentment. In any way he can, he entices us to remain in our pain and bitterness and, above all, not to see it as sin. He wants to deceive us into shrouding our wounds with a cape of respectability, perhaps to honor ourselves with a badge of recognition: Victim of the Year.

Can't you hear Satan's negative line? "These little emotions are mere nothings," he whispers. "Just deny them. They don't begin to compare with the BIG SINS, adultery or murder. Besides, after what happened to you, you have a right to feel the way you do."

If we fall for the enemy's line, we play right into his hand. His strategy is to immobilize us by causing us to harden our hearts. If he can do that, then he can frustrate God's master plan for the whole world, which is nothing less than expressing His love through His believers.

## A Way of Escape

The Good News is that we don't have to be stuck with blind eyes and hard hearts. We can move beyond the pain and bitterness. Why? Because God has provided a way of escape.

Listen closely to the Father's heart through the encouraging words of the apostle Paul:

> No temptation has overtaken you but such as is common to man; and God is faithful, who will not allow you to be

tempted beyond what you are able, but with the temptation will provide the way of escape also, that you will be
able to endure it (1 Cor. 10:13, *NASB*).

Essentially, Paul is pointing out two things here. First, that we
are tempted. That's the fact. And second, that God has made an
escape for us from every temptation. That's the hope.

Once more *Strong's Concordance* helps clarify. It cites the
Greek word translated "escape" as meaning "foot." Yes, as surely
as God made a way through the wilderness, He has made a way
for us today. Centuries ago, as Joshua stood hesitantly outside the
Promised Land, God encouraged him with a powerful promise: "I
will give you every place where you set your foot, as I promised
Moses" (Josh. 1:3).

Hear the depth of those words. They are our marching orders
even today! God is saying to us, "I want to give you dominion
over the enemy in your life. I want you to walk victoriously in
your land. Even as Joshua could walk victoriously in his land,
even as he could push his enemies aside and take possession of
what I had promised him, so can you."

God has given us authority over the things that cause our feet
to stumble and our hearts to hurt. He has given us a way to walk
out of our hurts and wounds.

His way of escape? Forgiveness.

But he involves us in the process. He honors our will. We
must make the choice to accept His way.

## Forgiveness Isn't Easy

Forgiving others is not easy. Someone has said that forgiveness is
love's toughest work and love's biggest risk. The act itself is simple, but because hurts occur within a storm of complex emotions, we rarely feel like doing it. Think about it: Who really
feels like forgiving someone who has inflicted pain in his life?

Who feels like being vulnerable when she's been the recipient of an unfair act? After all, if you've had a brush with a porcupine, you don't turn around and embrace the creature!

In her book *Something More*, Catherine Marshall underscores this concept:

> The love God demands can only be the gift of God. Yet He cannot give us that gift so long as bitterness and resentment have slammed shut the door of the heart and unforgiveness stands sentinel at the door lest love open and enter. Forgiveness is God's precondition to love.[3]

Most of us would choose to run the other way, find a place to lick our wounds and stay closed off to those who hurt us. We might even plot how we can get back at them. When we hear a story such as Julie's, we want to shout, "Hey, wait a minute! This is unfair and unkind. We need justice here!"

For years I made that same protest. "I've done everything I can do to make this marriage work! Howard needs to do something." Convinced that I was the innocent party, I believed he was the cause of my pain. So, in my hurt, I closed my heart to Howard and lived longer than I care to remember with pain and unforgiveness churning inside me.

Let's face it, forgiveness is not an automatic human reaction. The whole world says, "Find out who's guilty and make him pay." We want that person to hurt as deeply as he has hurt us. We can even want revenge.

Revenge? Yes, this reaction in natural man is as instinctive as breathing. Hurt? Injured? Then, strike back! Get even. Punish.

The Old Testament Mosaic covenant dealt with this aspect of human nature, even codifying the reaction specifically: "Fracture for fracture, eye for eye, tooth for tooth. As he has injured the other, so he is to be injured" (Lev. 24:20). On the surface this sounds like a mandate for retaliation, but it isn't.

In the ancient Near East, the practice was to kill the one who had caused injury. Thus, the Law of Moses, which sounds vindictive on the surface, actually aimed at limiting brutality to a manageable scope, not encouraging retribution.

By New Testament times, the Pharisees had interpreted the Law to mean that if a person injured another, he had to pay compensation equivalent to the damages caused.[4]

## Knowing God's Heart

Then Jesus burst upon the scene with a ministry showing what real love and forgiveness is all about. And it is not about law; it is about relationship.

Relationship. Jesus shows us throughout His teaching and preaching that this is what's on the Father's heart. Relationship is always the key with God.

That's why forgiveness is such a critical issue. Unforgiveness held in our hearts will always block our relationship with God, and when that relationship is blocked, all our relationships are affected.

Listen for this emphasis so clearly underscored in Jesus' teaching on the grassy hillside above the sea of Galilee near Capernaum.

Easy breezes sail off the water and up through the little knolls, moderating the temperature of an otherwise hot afternoon. The twelve, His inner circle of disciples, sit tightly wedged in the "front row seats," even leaning toward Jesus so as not to miss any words their beloved Master speaks. But there is a wider audience as well, others intent on hearing what this itinerant preacher has to say.

Like a good rabbi, Jesus sits down to teach. He begins by referring to the laws so familiar to His listeners. But within minutes, the familiar transitions to the unfamiliar and their ears quickly pick it up. Their heads are swimming with questions: *What kind of an approach is this?*

"You have heard that it was said, 'Do not murder, and anyone who murders will be subject to judgment.' But I tell you that anyone who is angry with his brother will be subject to judgment" (Matt. 5:21,22).

GOD'S HEART IS THAT WE GIVE LOVE
WITHOUT LOOKING FOR SOMETHING IN
RETURN. IT IS LOVE WITHOUT HOOKS.

*Angry? But come on, that's just a garden-variety everyday emotion. Everybody gets mad once in awhile.* Puzzled looks are exchanged, some clearing of throats, a little elbowing and lots of muttering.

Jesus, however, keeps on talking. "If you are offering your gift at the altar and there remember that your brother has something against you, leave your gift there in front of the altar. First go and be reconciled to your brother; then come and offer your gift" (Matt. 5:23,24).

Heads bob back in shock and comments fly. "This is ridiculous! If someone's hurt you, it's up to them to make the first move to reconcile."

For those so schooled in the rigors and traditions of the Law, Jesus' words sound like impossible gibberish. But His aim is neither to confuse them nor to give an innovative twist to the laws they already know.

He has come to show them one thing: the Father's heart of love. This is a love that impacts others with genuine mercy and heartfelt forgiveness. A love that brings life and healing in relationships. That nourishes and builds up. This is the message of the kingdom of God.

The Pharisees were majoring in the "outward" while God was calling for the "inward." Not law, form and traditions, but love, mercy and grace for relationships.

The gist of Jesus' teaching is revolutionary to His hearers. "Go deeper than the letter of the Law," He says. "Pray for your enemies; don't kill them. Forgive those who hurt you; don't seek revenge. Break out of your legalistic straitjackets. Watch how I eat with taxpayers and sinners; you go out and do the same. Throw open the doors of your heart and love!"

## Forgiveness Without Hooks

God's priority as expressed by Jesus is undeniably clear. Listen again to His commandment:

'Love the Lord your God with all your heart and with all your soul and with all your mind.' This is the first and greatest commandment. And the second is like it: 'Love your neighbor as yourself.' All the Law and the Prophets hang on these two commandments (Matt. 22:37-40).

God's heart is that we give love without always looking for something in return. It is love without hooks.

But how do you do this if you're like Julie, deeply wounded by a husband's unfair treatment? Or if you've been beaten and absent from your family for several years like the Beirut hostages in the early '90s, or held captive and mistreated like POWs from various wars?

How do you forgive those well-meaning parents, who in their inability to love well caused painful hurts? How do you forgive someone who has abused, even brutalized you? What is the answer?

We seem to be between a rock and a hard place.

On one hand, Scripture leaves no loopholes in admonishing us to forgive. "And when you stand praying, if you hold anything against anyone, forgive him, so that your Father in heaven may forgive you your sins" (Mark 11:25).

On the other hand, within ourselves, we don't have what it takes to leap over the hurdles of our hurts and offer forgiveness. Has God really called us to an impossible task?

Yes! Without a doubt. We are called to do something we cannot do. And, like the Israelites, whom God allowed to be humbled and proved in the wilderness, the sooner we know the depth of our inability to forgive, the better.

## The Work of God

One day following counseling, an impelling awareness of my need to forgive hit me full bore as I sat again at the kitchen table with my Bible. God was pressing me about this issue and, undeniably, I had a ways to go. I read and reread and cross-referenced Scriptures that spoke of forgiveness, many of them very familiar passages. I saw others with new clarity and focus—and imperative. And there at my table I literally raised my hand in surrender. My "poor me," unforgiving attitude plainly did not align itself with the Word of God.

Sure, during our counseling, my relationship with Howard was growing stronger and more open all the time. But when he answered me too abruptly or lost his temper over what I thought was "nothing," it was like I hit the brakes. Edges of the old anger crept back in; I reached for my old scorecard of his failures.

I didn't always move forward and forgive him. My heart told me I should, but I didn't. I withdrew, waiting and hoping Howard would come and apologize to me first. I wasn't proud of my reaction, but that's where I was—stuck.

I thought I wanted to love and forgive, to set aside my own restraints and expectations, but somehow when it came right down to letting Howard "go free," I dragged my heels. Sure, I could say the words, "I forgive you," but inside I kept waving a flag of rightness over my heart. And nothing moved past this obstacle.

Talk about ambivalence! A part of me yearned to walk up to a chalkboard, list Howard's failings, then pick up an eraser and rub out everything with delighted abandon.

But another part of me wanted to negotiate, remind him of my needs, and then make a deal.

I can't count the times Marilyn and Dick told me, "What leaves a heart reaches a heart." That profound little axiom was certainly true in this instance. For my words to Howard may have sounded all right, but when forgiveness is as measured and reluctant as mine was, the true feelings overrule what is said every time.

The harder I tried, the more I seemed to fail. Instead of swimming downstream in the River of Forgiveness, I was trapped in a lagoon, paddling in circles with no outlet in sight. I needed rescuing!

But no white knight rode triumphantly into my kitchen that day as I sat reading the Scripture that had corralled me with its clarity. No chariot descended from the sky to whisk me away from my disturbing dilemma. Yet help did come via a verse in John's Gospel. At last, the antidote for my poverty of spirit. Listen to it:

This is the work of God, that you believe in Him whom He has sent (John 6:29, NASB).

We often interpret this verse to mean that it is *our* effort that brings us to a place of belief, when in fact it is always the work of God that produces faith. One day the emphasis for me was on the first portion of that Scripture: "This is the work of God."

The difference in emphasis opened my eyes to a whole new understanding of how God undertakes for us. Our entire walk with Him is because of a work of God. Our belief, our faith, forgiveness of others—it is all possible only because God is working in our hearts.

Where had I been all my life? Why had I thought I could produce anything on my own that didn't have the shape of some kind of condition? I could no more manufacture forgiveness that would touch Howard at the heart level than I could create a prize-winning rose bush.

God alone can do the work. He is the Source.

He who offered the living water to the Samaritan woman would do it again for this woman who, despite all her study, had flunked Basic Forgiveness.

You can't give away something you don't have, something that's not in your heart. But I sure gave it a good try. I knew I ought to forgive Howard. Yet all I did when I had tried to forgive him was what our pastor calls "energizing the flesh." It's more like spinning your wheels in snow. You wear down your tires and you go nowhere.

## God at Work

One afternoon, Dick posed a hard question about my relationship with Howard. "Jane, why do you continually go back to his behavior? Why can't you let go and forgive him completely?"

I knew immediately what Dick was talking about, but I couldn't give him an answer. I didn't know why my attempts floundered, why unconditional forgiveness was not flowing out of me for Howard.

Dick pressed in with another approach. "Okay then, let's talk about your relationship with your father."

That was easy. I could answer without a second thought. "We were very close. Like two peas in a pod. I always respected him as a man of God."

Dick wanted a fuller picture. "Do you ever recall a time when you hopped up in his lap and he gave you hugs and kisses?"

I scrambled for a memory, for an instance I could remember. But there was none. Thick silence fell over the table as the true picture of my relationship with Dad dawned on me. I couldn't recall times like Dick was describing. All I could remember was that there was never time for hugging and kissing. Reality flashed into focus like I'd never seen it before.

Dick broke the silence with his matter-of-fact statement. "Jane, you have some very strong feelings toward your dad. Negative ones."

*Negative feelings?* My mind drew a blank. The only feelings I was aware of were ones of admiration and esteem for Dad as a man of God. "No," I protested, "I really loved him."

"Well, if you really want to be released from the emotional pain and unforgiveness you're carrying, you'll need to identify these feelings. In the next few days, if some old memories start surfacing, just start talking about them. I'm sure Howard will listen."

Marilyn added her encouragement to this assignment. "Talking doesn't create feelings, Jane. The feelings are already there. But talking will help bring them to the surface so you can deal with them."

Marriage and family counselor H. Norman Wright sheds light on the impact fathers have on daughters:

> Like it or not—your father has made a lasting impression on you. Whether he was close or distant, present or absent, cold or warm, loving or abusive, your father has left his mark on you. Your father is still influencing your life today—probably more than you realize.[5]

Sure enough. One evening a few days later, an old memory of my dad came to mind. Nothing overwhelming, but tangible enough that I knew it was a point to move on. I asked Howard if he'd come upstairs because I needed to talk about something important and I needed him to listen.

We went into the den. I sat in my rocking chair, gently pushing my feet back and forth against the floor, enough to sustain the movement of the big chair. Howard perched on the blue daybed, tapping his foot lightly on the rug. I started talking and, as I did, real feelings cut loose from their moorings like ships blown helplessly out to sea. My voice wavered as I described a painful childhood memory.

Howard, who at this point was uncomfortable when feelings were shared, immediately began fidgeting with a book lying on the bed, flipping it nervously open and shut and doodling with his fingers across the cover.

*He's not interested.* My old instant reaction surged to the fore. He coughed, then cleared his throat, and rubbed his arm as if looking for a tight muscle to massage. Clear signals to me. I vacillated between knowing I should keep talking to touch the depth of the struggle within me, and the old belief that I should be quiet because no one really had time to listen to what I had to say anyway.

Finally, I stopped in mid-sentence. "Howard, I feel like you're not even interested in what I'm saying."

"Oh, for crying out loud, I'm tired of being picked at for every little thing." Angry, his face turned red and he moved to leave the room.

I stood up, tight and stiff. My face, too, was warming with anger. Tears rolling down my cheeks, I raised my voice to answer back. "That's just how it is with men. They really don't care about women and children." Still louder I finished my attack. "They can't give them the time of day." Now overcome in full-blown sobs, I sank back into the rocking chair and let the floodgates open.

Someone observing our scene from the outside wouldn't have given us a gold star for our attitudes. Raised voices, tears and stormy exits from a room are hardly the ingredients of a happy weekend. Unless....

Unless the observer perchance knew something about the power of the resurrected Lord Jesus. How He dispatches the Holy Spirit, with infinite accuracy, to focus directly on our wounded spirits and pain-clogged hearts, to open us for His loving, tender healing and allow His forgiveness to do its work.

The vow I'd made as a child, that no man would ever hurt me like my dad hurt my mother, came echoing back to my remembrance. I heard my own voice repeat the judgment I'd made against all men.

Including Howard.

matt. 18: 21-35

# $\mathscr{M}$ERCY $\mathscr{T}$RIUMPHS

A vow made in childhood. Who would have guessed that a statement blurted out in hurt and anger could lodge in one's belief system, silently sabotaging relationships years later? Yet it happened to me.

When I said those strong words, "No man will ever hurt me like Dad hurt Mother," it was as if I immediately donned dark glasses and, from that moment on, viewed all men from an injured perspective.

Out of hurt and anger, I had made a judgment against men. Howard, of course, took the brunt of it. In a sense, I'd imprisoned him, locked him up by the long-standing conviction I held toward men.

Now, at last, I genuinely wanted to make things right with Howard. I wanted our relationship to be warm and open, yet somehow I could not seem to forgive him at a heart level.

Little did I know that every time I drove down the road to Forgiveness—even with the best of intentions—there was an unseen boulder blocking my way: My childhood judgment wouldn't let me pass through. Try as I might to move ahead, the judgment I'd made years before stopped me every time.

I began to see myself a failure as a forgiver. "I seem stuck at this same place, unable to really forgive Howard," I sighed one afternoon as I sat at Dick and Marilyn's table.

Dick nodded knowingly. "I understand how you feel. It's like a man trying to buy a $400 suit with $10 in his pocket." He continued with specific help. "Jane, let the Word of God speak to you."

Leaning back in his chair, Dick slowly and deliberately quoted from a passage in Luke's Gospel: "Be merciful, just as your Father is merciful. Do not judge, and you will not be judged. Do not condemn, and you will not be condemned. Forgive, and you will be forgiven" (Luke 6:36,37).

He paused briefly, then added his explanation. "The definition of mercy here is, 'Don't judge, don't condemn. But forgive.' This is mercy in action. Before you can give mercy and forgiveness to another, you must first apply this principle to your own life."

His words touched me as powerful messengers of hope. I knew I was hearing truth that would ultimately free me. I closed my eyes and nodded in silence, wanting every word to impact my heart.

Dick continued. "Jane, stop judging yourself. Stop condemning yourself and begin accepting God's forgiveness."

Marilyn looked me directly in the eye and beamed unmistakable encouragement. "This is a rich concept, Jane. Let it sink in for a few days."

And it did. Not only in the next few days, but also in the weeks and months to come.

## Understanding Mercy

For a long time I'd been trying to do the "right thing," trying to forgive Howard. But there was always that unseen boulder in my heart blocking my best efforts. God's Word, however, was at work, dismantling all the obstacles in my way.

In order to forgive unconditionally, as the father in Jesus' parable forgave his wayward son, I needed to quit judging myself and to embrace God's approach to forgiveness. And it begins with mercy.

Mercy—that's the front-runner of forgiveness.

Often we have a sentimental picture of mercy. A kind of feeling sorry for oneself or others. But God's definition of mercy is much more pointed toward redemptive action. His mercy sees through the eyes of understanding and compassion. It doesn't judge or condemn; it forgives.

Let me tell you a little story that beautifully illustrates mercy:

He was just a little boy whose mother took him to church every Sunday. Week after week, face scrubbed, hair slicked in place, he sat stiffly in the hard pew next to her. For him it was only a matter of routine, a duty, a habit, a have-to.

*If this is God's house*, he thought, *why isn't God home?* The little boy couldn't connect with a God who seemed as far away and uncaring as his sea captain father. Nor could he connect with a Jesus whom he saw in life-size marble statuary at several points around the church.

None of it made any sense to him. None of it touched him. Nothing registered. Well, almost nothing.

Every year, just before Easter, he remembered Jesus' dying words from the cross: "Father, forgive them, for they do not know what they do" (Luke 23:34, *NKJV*). Incredible, unforgettable words.

*No one but God could forgive like that.* That thought gripped this young boy's heart and never left him. He could tune out "religion," but he could not dismiss the possibility of this kind of love—a love that, in the face of death, wore the face of forgiveness.

It took years and his own desperate need, but at age 34 he found his answer: He, too, could know this kind of love—through a relationship with Jesus.

We see mercy abounding in Jesus' ministry. He encountered people caught in the grip of sin, blaming others, even hating themselves for their predicament. And yet, He didn't judge them. Instead, He mercifully extended healing and forgiveness.

He was a perfect picture of what the Scripture says: "Mercy triumphs over judgment!" (Jas. 2:13).

## Looking at Judgments

In order to experience mercy and apply it to my life, I had to begin looking at the judgments I'd made. Judgments toward myself and others.

Examine with me for a moment the anatomy of a judgment.

Something or someone hurts us and the pain of that incident wounds our heart. Our natural reaction to pain is anger, and this anger forms a hard layer over our pain. Judgments follow, sealing in our pain and anger deep within our heart.

As time passes, with each hurtful experience we have, we add evidence to substantiate the judgments we've made. Sometimes these judgments become all-encompassing. We paint all politicians, all reporters, all car salesmen, all teachers, all TV evangelists with the same brush of judgment. Objectivity vanishes. From then on, we operate from our base judgment, appraising them with, "That's the way they are."

What is a judgment?

*opinions vs. truth*

- A judgment is an opinion we hold as truth. It is not based on fact, for we have no way of knowing another person's heart or the things he has experienced. Even if our judgment were 99.9 percent accurate, it would still

164

be incomplete. That's why God has said, "You leave the judging to Me."

- Judging is based on what we see. We label others by their outward behavior. "She is cold." "He is indifferent."
- Judgments cause us to prejudge people: "I just know she won't approve of my choice" or "They aren't going to like me."
- Judgments put others down to make us look or feel better.
- Judgments lack mercy or forgiveness.
- Judgments feed on others' weaknesses or faults.

Judging is cruel. It is a destructive, sinful behavior. What are the results of judgments?

Because judgments are poisonous, they affect everything they touch, polluting, corrupting, crippling and finally destroying. They bind people, hampering the work of God in their lives. Families have been ruined by judgments. Churches have been split by them and ministries destroyed by them.

Judgments bring death, not life.

## Apply Mercy, Not Judgment

Over and over in the New Testament we read instances where Jesus illustrates His heart for mercy. One of my favorites is the story of the woman with the alabaster jar recorded by Matthew, Mark and John.

Recall the scene. Jesus is at a private gathering at the home of Simon the Leper. Into this little group bursts an uninvited woman with an alabaster bottle of perfume. Oblivious to the indignant reactions of the disciples, she pours her costly perfume over Jesus' head in a gesture of love and admiration.

The disciples immediately label this woman's actions as foolish. According to them, she had wasted the bottle's expensive contents. The perfume should have been sold and the money given to the poor. They missed seeing her motive—loving Jesus—and judged her on the spot.

Not so Jesus. He looked at the heart of this woman who had wet His feet with her tears, kissed them and poured perfume over them—and He did not judge her for wasting the costly oil. Instead, He commended her lavish love. (See Matt. 26:6-13.)

Mercy triumphed over judgment.

In another setting, a contemporary one, I also experienced the triumph of mercy over judgment for myself.

It happened with my friend Georgia. It seemed to me during several discussions together, she disagreed with me or even countered what I said with another point of view. I felt she was not really open to hearing my heart. Finally, one day when this happened again, I made a quiet judgment: Georgia always disagrees with me.

With the judgment came a decision: I would no longer try to have a relationship with her. You see, when I made that judgment, a barrier came up between us. And that's exactly what judgments do. While in a sense they protect us, at the same time they keep us from having relationships with others. You cannot have a deep, open relationship with a person you are judging.

I continued being pleasant and friendly with Georgia. On the surface, all appeared well until one day when a group of friends were together and everyone began expressing their love and encouragement to her.

She started to cry. "I appreciate your words, but why don't I feel your love?" With tears rolling down her cheeks, she looked searchingly at all our faces.

I knew as soon as the words were out of her mouth that I held a piece of this puzzle. At that moment, I had a choice to make. I needed to be honest with her. Could I do it? Or was being right more important to me than having a relationship with her? Was I willing to step over my self-righteousness? Would I continue in my commitment to having open, honest, real relationships?

I moved toward her and reached for her hand. "Georgia, I need to tell you that I judged you and closed my heart to you awhile ago. Because I was hurt, I decided to back away from our relationship. Please forgive me for closing my heart and judging you."

THE GLORIOUS PART OF BEING MERCIFUL,

OF NOT JUDGING, OF FORGIVING, IS THAT

WE BEGIN TO SEE WITH NEW EYES—

TO SEE AS JESUS SEES.

By taking total responsibility for my own actions, grace and forgiveness flowed. Georgia didn't know what the wall was; she only felt it. But it came down the moment forgiveness replaced the judgment.

From that day on, love has flowed freely between us.

## Seeing with New Eyes

The glorious part of being merciful, of not judging, of forgiving is that we begin to see with new eyes. Talk about sight for the blind! It was like God's unfolding miracle to me.

Remember my outburst about "all men"? A moment of great release came in the next counseling session after I reported the incident to Dick and Marilyn. We began looking at the vow I'd taken as a young child. I could see clearly, not only the vow, but the judgment and the crippling effect it had in my relationship with Howard. I had, in a sense, bound him, because I saw him as a man—like all others—who would hurt me.

We talked briefly about my need to forgive my father and Howard and to release all men from the judgment I had against them. Dick said, "Jane, you need to bring this to the Lord." He began leading me through a prayer of forgiveness, and as I spoke, deep pain welled up in me and began surging through me. Deep, deep pain.

I would have to call the experience a "divine exchange." As the excruciating pain was released, a depth of forgiveness such as I have never known swept over me. It was like someone took a gigantic eraser and totally wiped out everything on a huge blackboard, and then beckoned billowy waves of compassion to roll gently over me.

I thought of my mother, my dad, of Howard, and I wanted to shout at the top of my lungs, "I understand! I understand! I forgive you." Surely this must be how Jesus feels. I was so in touch with our Lord's compassion, His incredible love that only wants to reach out to us in our need. Nothing in me wanted to withhold forgiveness or mercy.

Within the next week, Mother became ill. Dad had died seven years before and she was alone. Late one night, Howard and I rushed over to her apartment and drove her to the hospital. She sat next to Howard in the front seat, and I sat in the back, my arm wrapped across her shoulders. Words of love came pouring spontaneously from my mouth. "Mom, have you any idea how much you've done for me? So many wonderful things. Do you know how much I love you?"

There was no need to spell out the events of the past in specifics. The work in my heart was finished, and she could feel my unrestrained love for her.

By the next evening she was gone. And I was a daughter, grieving again at the loss of a parent, but infinitely grateful for what God had done in my heart.

I was also beginning to see Howard with new eyes. Howard, whom I'd judged as uncaring and hard-hearted, began to look like a different person to me. Especially one particular summer evening.

We were standing on our front porch saying good-bye to our supper company when we heard our cat crying for help. A real wail of distress. "Howard, could you see about the cat? Sounds like it's stuck up in the cedar tree." A cat lover, I couldn't bear the thought of our cat trapped all night, cold and frightened.

Nonchalant, Howard laughed. "Hey, the cat got itself up the tree and it can get itself down. You'll see it on our doorstep tomorrow morning looking for food." I heard him chuckling all the way to the family room where he turned on the TV to catch the late news. *He's coldhearted.* The old judgment popped back into my mind.

I headed upstairs, crawled wearily into bed, disappointed that Howard didn't care enough to make some kind of rescue effort. Then I heard another noise—a ladder scraping against the side of the house. I sat up in bed, pushed aside the louvered shutter and peered through the window. There was Howard, out in the midnight air, up the 16-foot ladder, leaning his tall frame against the tree and calling, "Here kitty, kitty." I saw him cradle the terrified cat in his strong arms, inch slowly down the ladder and pet the trembling creature as he carried her lovingly to the garage.

I turned my face to my pillow and let the tears flow. What a tenderhearted man I'm married to. And what a wonderful Father we have who helps us release our judgments and receive His love.

I dried my eyes and sat up to greet Howard when he came trooping in the door and up to bed. "Come here, Howie," I beckoned, gesturing to my side of the bed. As he sat down, I took his hand in mine and said, "I really love you."

In ourselves, we don't have the ability to see with new eyes, even when we try to do the "right thing." It is only the supernatural work of the Holy Spirit that plummets to the depths of our hurt, anger and pain to dislodge that which blocks our love.

However, when the Spirit does the work, we see as Jesus sees.

# Forgiveness: The Foundation for Continuing Relationships

At the Wednesday men's meeting at our church, Howard had shared how he'd had a bad attitude toward Jeff, how for years their relationship was riddled with arguments and judgments, particularly after Jeff had gotten into the drug scene. Now he wanted a fresh start with Jeff, but he felt awkward going directly to him and bringing up the past.

"Why not write him a letter? Tell him exactly how you feel. Let him hear your heart." The pastor's words gave him hope and a way to communicate the love he wanted to express to Jeff.

Howard composed three drafts, all outlining Jeff's problems and blaming him for his actions. The wastebasket claimed all of them. The fourth try was a winner—a long two-page, single-spaced letter enumerating the ways he had been wrong in his harsh judgments and his failure to understand how Jeff was struggling. When he got to the end, he wrote two lines expressing how he had also been hurt by Jeff. In simple words he asked for forgiveness.

The letter reached Jeff a day later. Surprised to be getting a long letter from his dad, Jeff could hardly believe what he was reading. But the words deeply touched him, and their relationship, long stalemated by negative jabs and persistent arguments, was restored. Forgiveness did its work. Mercy triumphed again!

At another point, Howard went to Lisa and asked forgiveness for not showing her the kind of love she needed during her growing-up days. Again, owning his own actions, he moved in the grace of Jesus, and she, too, responded with acceptance and forgiveness.

As I watched these events unfold in such natural and loving ways, I was amazed...and humbled. God, who had led me into my prayer closet years ago, had faithfully answered the prayers I'd prayed for Jeff and our family. Not only was Jeff doing well, now married and enjoying his family, but all our relationships were being touched and restored.

## *Forgiving the Debt*

It's hard to describe the impact of what was evolving in our marriage and in our family. Everything was changing as walls of self-protection and judgment crumbled around us. However, there was one more wall to go—the Jericho of our marriage.

I'd been at lunch with three longtime friends. Over dessert, Marie mentioned that the Lord had spoken to her through the story of the ungrateful servant in Matthew 18. Remember that passage, where Peter asks Jesus how many times he needs to forgive his brother when he sins against him? The law allowed seven, but Jesus said it was seventy times seven. Limitless.

And then Jesus tells the parable. One man who owes the king ten thousand talents is brought before him, unable to pay. Threatened with the loss of his wife, children and goods, he pleads for time enough to pay back everything. Touched by his plight, the merciful master does more than extend the time, he cancels the entire debt for the anxious man.

However, when the debtor is approached by a fellow servant who pleads for mercy over a far lesser debt, he grabs him, chokes him and demands repayment. He who had received such generous mercy refuses to give any to the next person. Angered, the servant's master turns him over to the jailers to be tortured until the full debt is paid. Jesus concludes with stern words about the cost of unforgiveness: "This is how My heavenly Father will treat each of you unless you forgive your brother from your heart" (Matt. 18:35).

I drove home from that luncheon deeply moved by our discussion of canceling debts. Howard and I had been learning so much about forgiveness, but now I sensed one more step needed to be taken. Not only are we to forgive others for what they have done, but we are to forgive them for what we perceive they "owe" us.

In our relationships with others, some of our expectations are healthy and legitimate. Not only those for security and significance, but also expectations of relationship, respect and responsible behavior. This is the debt we owe one another. It is love in action. "Owe no one anything except to love one another," declared Paul (Rom. 13:8, *NKJV*).

But what if after years of disappointment, we come to realize those legitimate desires will never be perfectly fulfilled by imperfect human beings? The only thing left is to forgive the debt—those things that were legitimately owed to us.

I realized I was to forgive Howard for what I believed he owed me—past and present—and release him from any future expectations of perfect behavior I might have of him.

The Lord had my attention on this! "Lord, set up the right time to talk with Howard," I prayed.

Although I'd often forgiven Howard for the past, I still communicated the feeling to him that he could never fully repay what I felt I'd lost. In fact, I'd carried the debt over into the future. Because of this, he could never be free.

Later that week, I was working upstairs in my office when Howard came in and sat on the daybed. He'd come to ask my forgiveness for something he'd done. This was the time. I knew I needed to bring up the issue of canceling the debt.

Howard had previously told me that he never felt worthy of being forgiven. And now I saw that although I'd forgiven him for the past and said clearly, "Let's pick up and go on," he continued to get the feeling from me that he still owed for the future.

"Howie, I've been holding you responsible for a long time for a debt I felt you owed me. As of this day, I am totally releasing you."

The Lord's presence descended quietly into the room in a way we'd never experienced. We held each other and wept as we prayed. All debt was now canceled.

As far as I was concerned, that day the enemy was stripped of his power to wreak havoc in our home and our marriage. For two full days following the canceling of the debt, Howard sat in his rocking chair in the family room, utterly drained and too weak to move. He wept quietly as he sat almost immobilized, except for his gentle rocking back and forth in his chair.

Something powerful had happened in the spiritual realm, and the Lord was literally touching Howard with His healing power in a new depth of release.

## A Special Rose

One Saturday afternoon, shortly after the canceling of the debt, we were painting a bedroom and we began to talk about the painful patterns we had set up in our marriage.

We both agreed that our pattern of relating to each other had been negative from the moment we "brought in the baggage" with our marriage vows. I came into marriage with voracious needs for love and acceptance resulting from the pain of my childhood. I came with great expectations that Howard would not only meet my needs, but become the source of life to me.

Howard, on the other hand, came with his own needs for love and significance. He also came with fears that he couldn't measure up to my expectations. Early in the marriage, he felt intimidated by my demands. The more I wanted, the more he backed off emotionally, distancing himself safely at arm's length.

That afternoon, paint brushes in hand, we were able to talk objectively about our relationship as we casually painted around the little room. Howard spoke vulnerably from his heart. He talked about insecurities he'd struggled with since childhood, the tremendous pressure and disappointments he'd felt at work when we were first married, and how panic gripped him at having the responsibility of a family.

"I guess that all added up to my becoming so unreachable," he said, as he brought his explanation to a close. Honest and straightforward, his words seemed to hang in the air, suspended momentarily for me to fully grasp.

Tears rolled down my cheeks. I put down my brush and reached for a tissue. There was nothing to say. I now understood why Howard had become so distant. At last I had heard him with my heart.

Again, in our vulnerability, the Holy Spirit's presence tangibly enveloped us, paint brushes and all.

Like the Israelites who marked significant milestones with a memorial stone, we felt as if we needed to mark the end of that painful era in our marriage. We closed down our little decorating project, cleaned up and headed for the neighborhood nursery.

Our eyes lit simultaneously on a beautiful yellow rose bush. We grinned. We knew we'd found our special rose.

At home, by the side of the house, Howard dug the hole. I brought over the bag of fertilizer and a bucket of water, and together we gingerly placed our "memorial stone" into the garden soil, tamping it in tightly around the roots. Our soil-covered hands met and squeezed over the new plant.

"I can't wait to smell the rose," Howard said, wiping away a tear.

"I can't either, Howie," I added, doing my own planting—a kiss on his forehead.

Howard and I were learning to walk in the truth of God's Word, and this lovely yellow rose would blossom each year to become the tangible symbol that we would no longer be reaping from our foolish ways. Instead God would be producing the fruit of love in us—His way.

# $\mathcal{T}$HE $\mathcal{J}$OURNEY TO $\mathcal{L}$OVE

Maybe the book is on your bookshelf, too. My copy is dog-eared, highlighted, well worn. Over the years, whenever I reach for Hannah Hurnard's timeless Christian allegory, *Hind's Feet on High Places*, I am reminded that I've not been alone on my journey toward love. I wonder how many others have bent over Hurnard's pages and found—like a mirror—their own reflection as I have. How many others could say with me, "That's my story"?

I can relate so easily to little Much-Afraid, crippled and disfigured, on her winding one-way trek from the Valley of Humiliation to the High Places of her Shepherd. It wasn't a health club billboard or the promise of a long, reviving soak in a hot tub that spurred her on through setbacks and successes. It was the dream that on those airy heights, she would finally be whole and free. Best of all was the promise that the seed of true love would at last be planted deep in her heart.

In my relationships with God, with Howard and with others, the Lord used many ways to bring me back to the same penetrating question he posed to Much-Afraid, a.k.a. Jane: "Has Love been planted in your heart?"[1]

And in many ways my answer was an echo of my limping storybook friend. "What is growing (in my heart) is a great longing to experience the joy of natural human love and to learn to love supremely one person who will love me in return."[2] But what about love with no return? What about love that just gives and doesn't wait for change? The kind with absolutely no guarantee against heartbreak?

## Love with Hooks

In our world, it seems only right. It seems only fair. *Give to get. Give to get.* So much of what we call "love" marches to that desperate, secret cadence.

Remember Valentine's Day in school? You saved your biggest and best valentine for that Special Person. Then, when the final tally came and you received only a generic penny card from him, a card like everyone else's, you wished you hadn't wasted your best on him. You felt embarrassed, even ashamed that you made yourself so vulnerable.

We so seldom have a clue that the valentine of love we hold out to others carries on its back the fine print of our expectations. We may really think we're being selfless. We might even feel safely justified when our expectations harden into steely demands. *But he's supposed to meet my needs. He's my husband, isn't he?*

I think we all love with hooks, and I'll tell you why I'm so sure of it. Because like our first parent Adam, our hearts have a reflex bent toward foolishness. In a sense, our hooks are innate; but as we grow, they become more polished and acceptable. Like a stubborn crease that persists even after numerous ironings, our hearts fold again and again around the core belief that we can live life on our own terms and make it work for us. It takes the Holy Spirit to convince us we can't.

Like all of us, I've tried countless subtle or not-so-subtle ways to take people hostage with the hooks of my love. It has happened whenever I've pulled people toward myself for my own purposes and benefit, not for their own good and certainly not for God's.

A hook is a behavior based in a belief and may be expressed in many ways. It may be a look, a feeling, a way of responding or not responding, a deeply buried expectation or a loudly proclaimed demand. For years I "hooked" Howard with my questions, wanting to elicit a particular feeling from him. I wanted him to see my needs—and change.

A lifetime of anxiously shaping and polishing our heart hooks can make us masters at trying to extract from others what we believe we must have to be happy. Sounds pretty calculated, doesn't it? But it becomes second nature, and we get to be such pros at it that we even deceive ourselves.

"Not me," you might say. But think: Don't you know the feeling? Your husband doesn't pick up on your well-placed clues that you wanted anniversary roses. Your best friend suddenly stops calling you and starts calling someone else. Your usually supportive boss passes you over and promotes the coworker you trained. Your teenager stares sullenly at the floor as you talk and shrugs off your affirming hug. Winds of war are blowing. Watch out, the war that the disciple James talked about may suddenly be rumbling inside you, threatening to kick into full gear.

War? What war? *The Amplified Bible* gives us a full description of this "internal" war:

What leads to strife (discord and feuds) and how do conflicts (quarrels and fightings) originate among you? Do they not arise from your sensual desires that are ever warring in your bodily members? You are jealous and covet [what others have] and your desires go unfulfilled; [so] you become murderers. [To hate is to murder as far as your hearts are concerned.] You burn with envy and anger and are not able to obtain [the gratification, the contentment, and the happiness that you seek], so you fight and war. You do not have, because you do not ask. [Or] you do ask [God for them] and yet fail to receive, because you ask with wrong purpose and evil, selfish motives. Your intention is [when you get what you desire] to spend it in sensual pleasures (Jas. 4:1-3).

We want. We need. We thirst. Like the woman at the well wanting to find love, our thirst is legitimate. It's what we reach for to quench it that is often so sadly off the mark.

This passage in James again reveals the foolish pursuits and beliefs that drive us—and the strife, quarrels and discord that are the result of our own demands for others to meet our needs. This Scripture clearly shows the turning of our hearts, the spiritual adultery of turning away from God for satisfaction elsewhere.

No one told us, but we began early, even as little children, thinking that people around us have the potential to fill the deepest places within us—if only we can convince them to do it.

I think Leah must have known something of that. As I read her story in Genesis 29, I cannot help but feel empathy for her. She, through no choice of her own, was relegated to second-place status in her marriage, and she tried desperately to make up for it.

Given deceptively in marriage to Jacob as a substitute for the more beautiful Rachel, Leah must have flinched at seeing the disappointment in her husband's eyes on their wedding morning. Her pain only intensified when Jacob married Rachel and, according to Scripture, "He loved Rachel more than Leah" (Gen. 29:30).

Hope flickered in her heart time and time again as God opened her womb. "It is because the Lord has seen my misery," she explained, poignantly adding, "Surely my husband will love me now" (Gen. 29:32).

Then after giving birth to two more sons, she voiced hope once more: "Now at last my husband will become attached to me" (Gen. 29:34).

She kept hoping, kept trying. How many times did she carry a new son hopefully out into the pale light of morning? How many times did she search for the spark of delight and approval in Jacob's eyes, the tender look he reserved for Rachel alone? She tried so hard and she was so thirsty. Like us she must have been battle-weary, trapped by her own hooks in a contest she could never win. That was the same place I was when Dick leaned across the table and said, "Jane, why do you want Howard to change?" And later I knew the answer: "For me."

Loving with hooks closes us to God and to others. And what is more, it carries a high price. Our homes, our health, our children and our marriages are the casualties. There must be a better way.

## God's Ways Are Not Ours

Movie actor Burt Reynolds, known in years past for his playboy lifestyle, openly described his quest for love in a recent newspaper article. He recalled growing up in the South with the traditional saying, "No man is a man until his father tells him he is." To Burt that meant that someday when he was 30 or 40, his dad, the one he loved and respected and wanted to be loved by, would put his arms around him and say, "You know, you're a man now, and you don't have to do crazy things and get into fistfights and all that to prove you're a man. You don't have to prove anything. You're a man and I love you."

But Burt never got what he yearned for from his father. "We never hugged, we never kissed, we never said, 'I love you.' No, we never cried." Life was lonely without affection and affirmation. "I was desperately looking for someone who'd say, 'You're grown up, and I approve and love you, and you don't have to do these things anymore.' I was lost inside. I couldn't connect. I was incomplete.

*I didn't know then what I needed to know."* (Italics mine).

So many of us have struggled on the same journey to love. Longing to be accepted, looking for love, we set out on our journey using our own road map. We scramble up the hills of Love Me and down the valleys of Affirm Me and along the treacherous shoals of Give Me Life to get our needs met apart from God. To get—that's always the thrust of human love. That was my thrust for so many years.

Listen to the words of the Lord:

"For my thoughts are not your thoughts, neither are your ways my ways," declares the Lord. "As the heavens are higher than the earth, so are my ways higher than your ways and my thoughts than your thoughts" (Isa. 55:8,9).

I needed to learn that God's way was 180 degrees from my way. I never sat down at a drawing board, sketched out my approach to life and said, "Now, Jane, go for it. Win a husband, make a marriage, buy a house and thereby be happy." No, I simply went my own way, to get my needs met on my own terms because I followed the bent of my sinful heart, which is always diametrically opposed to God's ways.

Do you ever do things the hard way? Maybe just by mistake? Howard picked up our regular brand of tea the other day at a warehouse grocery where they sell products only in large quantities. Eager for a cup of tea, I ripped open the box. Rather than loose tea bags, I found each one enclosed in an individual package. I tore open one end, only to discover I'd also torn the tea bag inside, spilling out the loose tea. Flipping the package over, I noticed a little flap marked "Open here." I'd opened the tea the hard way, my way, and I'd reaped the consequences all over the floor.

God wants us to do it His way, a way rich beyond our wildest imaginations in its dimensions of love. The admonitions of Scripture, including the Ten Commandments, were never meant to hinder us or to stifle our personalities, but rather to show us the way to live life to the fullest. Jesus used the word "abundant." He said, "I have come that they may have life and that they may have it more abundantly" (John 10:10, *NKJV*). If we want this abundant life that God promises us, we have to go His way.

And when it comes to love, God has called us to walk in a way that is not natural to us. God's way of love is giving, not getting.

GOD'S WAY OF LOVE IS GENEROUS AND
OPEN. SO OPEN THAT HIS SON DIED
ON THE CROSS, HANDS NAILED OPEN
AND ARMS OUTSTRETCHED.

We think if we can get love then we'll be fulfilled and have love to give, but this is contrary to God's way of love.

Our "love" is divisive and filled with strife because it is self-directed; God's love always builds relationships. It has no conditions. Our "love" is careful, guarded and calculating, protecting our hearts at all costs; God's love is generous and open. So open that His Son died on the cross, hands nailed open and arms outstretched.

I recently asked women at a retreat in Texas to give me their definitions of love. They were quick to respond with words like "caring," "compassion," "kindness"—all good answers.

Then I shared with them my pastor's definition: "Love is openness, honesty and trust."

For a moment the room was silent. Then faces lit up as the women caught hold of the possibilities of this kind of love—a love that risks, a love that makes itself vulnerable. A love that is more than a feeling; it is a choice.

For little Much-Afraid, the path up the mountain to love often seemed like a backwards route. From the Valley of Humiliation, across the desert, on the shores of loneliness, into the forests of danger and tribulation, through floods and mists, even enduring silence from the Shepherd Himself, every inch of the arduous route went against her natural inclination to be safe and secure. And yet, somehow she did not turn back, even when she was asked to make the final sacrifice: to pull out the root of her own love, that God's love might be planted in its place. And much to her delight, she discovered that there is always more grace than suffering.

## Called to an Impossible Task

At the invitation of a friend, Carol Greenwood and I flew down to Florida in mid-January to concentrate on writing this book. Just as we were getting ready for bed one night, a loud boom thundered through the air and every light in the house went out. We were terrified.

For three long hours, we sat in the darkness with only a few flickering candles for light. Finally we dialed 911. Firemen answered our call and arrived to search the house. They tried to set our minds at rest: "It's a transformer knocked out by an electrical storm. Happens all the time around here. Nothing wrong in the house. Might as well relax."

*Relax?* We wanted the lights on!

That night, we had several choices for how to deal with the physical darkness. We could accept it, curse it or even convince ourselves that it really wasn't that dark after all. Still, the one thing we could not do was make it be light. Until the electricity flashed back on, it was going to be dark. We could jiggle plugs, flip switches, even shake the chandelier; but without electricity coming through the wires, all our efforts would be futile. Making it "be light" was an impossible task.

Jesus, too, it appears, has called us to an impossible task. Shortly before His crucifixion, He gave His disciples a new commandment:

Love one another. As I have loved you, so you must love one another. By this all men will know that you are my disciples, if you love one another (John 13:34,35).

A new commandment. A new standard of love. Through them! *Through us!* A foot-washing, laying-down-one's-life kind of love. Selfless, servant-like, a love that sings out across the weary world like a heavenly symphony, melting hearts, bringing hope out of despair and life out of death. A love that makes a difference—for eternity.

An impossible task? Yes. Meet Jane Hansen, total failure on the love assignment. She tried to flip switches and shake chandeliers in the guise of perfectly cooked meals, beautifully manicured flower beds and an impeccable house—and she could not get rid of the darkness. She could not graduate with a "Love Degree."

As you've seen, even my best efforts to show love were riddled with selfishness. Foolishness was the rudder of my life, motivating me to seek love on my terms. My heart cried for relationship—the very desire put there by God—but I wanted it for all the wrong reasons. Not to lay down my life for Howard, but to get filled up on his love. And what did God want? Nothing less than those fruitless "best efforts." He wanted the "thing" that stood between Jane and God. He wanted to be the source of my love. He wanted nothing to come between our relationship. In a sense, he wanted my "Isaac."

Remember the story? God's command to Abraham was pretty clear: "Take your son, your only son, Isaac, whom you love, and go to the region of Moriah. Sacrifice him there as a burnt offering on one of the mountains I will tell you about" (Gen. 22:2).

"But God, Isaac was your idea!" If it had been me, I would have protested loudly. "He represents your promise, your will. You ini-

tiated all this, and now you want me to put him on the altar?!"
Does this sound heartless and cruel? Unloving?

But, wait! God saw the bigger picture. He saw a man, the one
He had covenanted with to produce descendants as many as the
stars in the sky, and this man had begun to wrap his heart and life
around a person.

The test at the altar of Moriah was not only about obedience
to God, but also about God's desire to keep Abraham's heart solely focused on God Himself. Not a person. Not even a promise,
but God.

Our hearts are so easily turned aside. It isn't that we are not
to trust God's promises, but when the fulfillment of those promises stands between us and our relationship with God, we are in
danger of putting something above loving God. And He wants to
be wanted just for Himself.

That was also the test for little Much-Afraid. Could she give up
her human love for God's love? Ultimately that was my test, too.

I could not love as Jesus called me to any more than I could
force electricity through the wires of the Florida house  God was
calling me to put all my hopes and dreams of love and marriage
on the altar. Such a choice cuts across the fabric of our selfish,
sin nature. Death to self and all its demands! For Jesus to establish His way of relationship, the way of love and forgiveness, this
means death to every human effort or aspiration.

In her book *Adventures in Prayer*, Catherine Marshall writes,
"The cult of humanism in our day has trained us to believe that
we are quite adequate to be masters of our own destiny."[3]

But when it concerns loving like Jesus, forgiving like Jesus,
the truth is "Apart from me you can do nothing" (John 15:5).

John the Baptist told his followers, "A man can receive only
what is given him from heaven" (John 3:27). Loving like Jesus? Is
it possible? With our love, no.

But here's the hope: "What is impossible with men is possible with God" (Luke 18:27). He has already "poured out his love

into our hearts by the Holy Spirit" (Rom. 5:5) and longs to give that love away through us.

## Are We There Yet?

Station wagon loaded to the roof with sleeping bags, tent, food for the weekend and three super-eager kids crowded in the second seat, the five Hansens set out lumbering down the freeway.

As far as our kids were concerned, we couldn't reach the campsite fast enough. "Are we there yet?" Scott, our youngest and an especially avid camper, asked the question when we'd been on the road less than half an hour. But the chorus picked up rapidly from then on and continued in ten-minute intervals. "Hey Dad, how much farther to go?" "When are we going to get there, huh, Dad?"

Sometimes a bag of potato chips or a box of raisins handed to the second seat bought us a little time and staved off the nonstop questions, momentarily at least. These were kids who loved camping and they didn't move off track easily. Destination was never far from their minds.

It is never far from believers' minds, either. "Are we making headway?" "Are we getting closer?" "Do we arrive soon?" Destination looms pretty high on our list, the place where we can kick off our shoes and relax for the weekend in our spiritual tents by the fast-flowing waters. "How much longer till we're there?" Loving like Jesus? Forgiving like Jesus? When will we make it?

Have you ever noticed that, while the Bible shines its light on the hope of heaven, it doesn't center exclusively on our arrival? In fact, over and over it encourages us to move ahead, to press on, not to faint. Even to embrace the path. The Lord values the journey. It is "on the way" that He has opportunity to reveal His presence, to lovingly guide, to strengthen us, to provide what we need. In fact, the psalmist sounds almost like a travel agent waving goodbye to a departing traveler: "Blessed are those whose strength is in you, who have set their hearts on pilgrimage" (Ps. 84:5).

"Are we there yet?"

And where is there? *There* is heaven. As C. S. Lewis said, the life we know now is only the title page. Yet the now of this earth is where we learn the stuff of loving. In his book *Don't Waste Your Sorrows*, Paul Billheimer states, "It is important to remember that this life is a laboratory, an apprenticeship in which God is teaching His children agape love in preparation for rulership."[4] This is not where we arrive; it is where we practice.

Billheimer goes on to quote C. S. Lovett, writing, "Heaven is no place to raise kids."[5] Why? Heaven is not a place where we experience the trials and tests that produce growth. Earth is the place of learning; heaven is of an entirely different order.

## *Producing the Finished Product*

But wait. Are we saying that God stands over us, shaking His head, saying something like, "I wonder if they'll ever make it"? No, not at all. Let me illustrate.

A few years back, Bette, an interior designer friend, agreed to help me redo our master bedroom. We talked initially about colors and the look I wanted. Then a week or so later she appeared, dozens of samples in hand and an expectant look on her face. We sorted through her bag of samples and finally reached a decision on the look, feel and color of the new room. She spread everything out on the bed—carpet samples, paint swatches, fabric pieces—stood back with upraised hand, eyed the room and exuded, "Oh, I just love it. It's beautiful."

I couldn't see a thing except an old room in need of help and the contents of her sample bag. "Really?" Half-question, half-apprehension, my weak query disclosed my puzzlement.

"Oh, Jane, when I get a room this far, to me it's as good as finished."

Bette, with her expertise in interior design, could already see the end result. She was confident in her ability to create the

THE  JOURNEY  TO  LOVE

finished product. All I saw was walls that needed painting, a floor that needed fresh carpet and worn furniture that needed replacing. Nothing was changed and certainly not new. Yet, as far as Bette was concerned, once I had selected the interior decorator, counted the cost and decided to proceed, the result was guaranteed.

*How like God,* I pondered several days later. The same principle applies. He waits and lets us make the choice; He encourages us to count the cost and waits to be invited into the situation. Once these things "line up" then He, like Bette, can say, "It's as good as finished," fully confident in His ability to bring it forth.

In the New Testament, Abraham is described as a finished product. Paul writes, "Abraham believed God, and it was credited to him as righteousness" (Rom. 4:3). Nothing is mentioned of the flaws we read about in the Old Testament. Through it all, God was confident, not in Abraham's ability, but in His own to produce a man of God—a finished product.

He can do the same in you and me.

To carry the analogy further, the end result of my decorating project was that others have exclaimed over my beautiful room, the finished product. Invariably, they ask the same questions: "Was it terribly costly?" and "Tell me, who was your interior designer?"

## Love's Extravagance

An example of God's extravagant love toward us comes from a story told by internationally known Christian author and artist Joni Eareckson Tada.

"That Ken! So thoughtful." Red roses greeted Joni a week before Valentine's Day, an early gift from her husband, Ken. The roses in the living room were arranged in an elegant crystal vase. She loved them.

But there were more.

There were roses in the kitchen, too. And the bathroom counter was graced with one lovely bud. Roses in abundance. Fragrant, gorgeous roses all over the house! And Joni's next reaction? "This was a bit much....Expensive flowers at that. I was irked. It wasn't that I didn't appreciate [Ken's] gifts, it's just that nobody but our dog, Scruffy, would be in the house to enjoy the flowers."

Joni would be away on a speaking engagement and Ken would be fishing all weekend. No one in the house to enjoy the beautiful flowers. They'd be wasted. It seemed so extravagant to spend money like this.

Yet, as she thought about the ministry of love, she realized, "Love never thinks in terms of 'how little,' but always in terms of 'how much.'" Ken's own ministry to her was a perfect example: his daily sacrifices of love to fix her wheelchair, wash the dishes, turn her on her side, brew coffee before he left for work. "Loving his wife who cannot rub his back or fold his towels." According to Joni, "Love is extravagant in the price it is willing to pay, profuse, even wasteful in the time it is willing to give, the hardships it is willing to endure, and the strength it is willing to expend."[6]

Has it ever caught your attention how many ways God shows His extravagance? We need look no farther than nature to see his infinite assortment of animal and plant species, of colors, textures and forms. His artistry knows no bounds. Birds on every continent singing different songs, trees in every nation bending under different climates, geological masses enhancing the terrain of every continent—from towering mountains to deep canyons. A symphony in extravagance playing across the face of this planet, the praises of a Creator whose love keeps giving!

Like Joni, we so often squirm in the presence of such extravagance. I have had to learn to receive compliments and gifts with open hands. But my natural tendency is to think, *I don't deserve this. This is too much.* Pure love poured out without a way to reciprocate or without thought of the price tag touches all of us who have so long lived lives that measured out love to "the deserving" or those who can reciprocate.

How our Father wants us to receive and enjoy His extravagant love! Remember Joni and the roses? The ones she thought would be wasted on an empty house? Well, they were there waiting for her when she returned from her weekend away. Hear those moments in her own words:

> I wheeled through the front door, expecting the musty smell of a closed-up house. But I was in for a surprise. The buds had bloomed. Their fragrance filled the cold, dark rooms. And love was there, brightening our home with its sheer, wasteful extravagance.[7]

## A Lesson in Lavishness

Those present at Simon the Leper's house in Bethany were definitely uncomfortable at what they considered a wasteful display. In fact they were indignant when the woman with the alabaster jar broke it and poured the perfume over Jesus' head. The jar itself was costly. And the perfume? No dime store imitation. Likely *spikenard*, a fragrance costing a year's wages. Spilled over Jesus' head when it could have gone to the poor. *That's where it could have done some good!* they thought.

Rebukes came easily from those watching. Not just quiet comments, but harsh words. Except from Jesus. The recipient of the lavish expression of the woman's love responded with firmness. "Leave her alone. She has done a beautiful thing to me. Wherever the gospel is preached throughout the world, what she has done will also be told, in memory of her" (Mark 14:6,9).

What was it about this event that so arrested Jesus' attention? Could it have been that the woman's love wore no price tag? For her Lord, she would not count the cost. Even what might have been her nest egg, her retirement fund, her security—it was nothing in the face of honoring her Lord. And Jesus notes it for

THE WORLD SAYS, "PROTECT YOURSELF
AT ALL COSTS. YOU GAIN WHEN YOU GET."
THE TRUTH IS WHEN YOU OPEN YOURSELF
TO GIVE, YOU ALWAYS GAIN.

all time and all peoples: Here is a picture of the Father's love—right before our eyes.

Paul writes a strong prescription for love in his letter to the Ephesians:

> Be imitators of God, therefore, as dearly loved children and live a life of love, just as Christ loved us and gave himself up for us as a fragrant offering and sacrifice to God (Eph. 5:1,2).

Imitators of Christ. That's a hard act to follow. He gave His life. In what ways can that kind of love manifest itself in us?

One way I've been learning came from my experience in counseling. Do you recall how Dick challenged me to lay down my life for Howard? When I protested with the long list of things I'd done, he pointed out that love is not just doing things, it is giving yourself for another person.

Being open becomes the anchor of love. For while homemade pies may well be part of loving, God is after open hearts that will choose to lay down our preference for staying hidden or being right or running from relationships. Love is not just doing things for people; it is giving yourself. Genuine fulfillment comes when you give love. It is a paradox: Giving away love is what fills you up.

Radical? Yes. The whole world says, "Protect yourself at all costs. You gain when you get." The godly truth is when you open yourself to give, you always gain. The more you give, the more you come out of yourself—and begin to see the world as the Lord sees it.

## Treasure in Heaven

"All" is such an inclusive word. All. Everything. There's nothing left. Like when you close out your bank account and the clerk hands you a receipt that could just as well contain the words, "Now your money is all gone." The zero in front of you confirms it. *All* leaves no room for negotiating.

In a societal climate that panders to compromise and half-heartedness, "all" is an old-fashioned word. It means going over-board. Too far. Only country western music dares to croon something like, "I'm giving you all my life, all my love, all my self...."

Look for a moment at a biblical hall of fame of some folks who found something in their lives that prompted them to give their all. A poor widow comes by the Temple's treasury to put in her two copper coins. Jesus commends her in front of those who could outgive her a hundredfold. "All these people gave their gifts out of their wealth; but she out of her poverty put in all she had to live on" (Luke 21:4).

The hall of fame includes the man who found a treasure in the field, hid it and sold all he had to buy the field. (See Matt. 13:44.) And the merchant, looking for fine pearls, finds one of great value and sells all he has to secure it. (See Matt. 13:45.)

Hannah Hurnard's Much-Afraid, too, came on her journey up the mountain to the "all" of the altar. "Tie me down," she plead-ed, afraid still that her own fear might rise up at the last minute and resist the very thing her heart was crying for—to have her self-love all plucked out.

And then there was one who could not give all. In answer to the rich young ruler who inquired how he might find eternal life, Jesus said, "If you want the treasure in heaven, you must sell all." Those present might have heard Jesus say, "I have to have all of your heart." Then they watched as the man walked sorrowfully away, choosing his lifeless god over the God of life. (See Mark 10:17-22.)

What is a treasure? We know that pirates have killed for it. Kings have fought for it. Misers have hoarded it. It is precious. Rare. Valuable. A treasure has inestimable value; so much so, it hooks your heart and you will "sell out" to have it for yourself.

"For where your treasure is, there your heart will be also" (Matt. 6:21). Jesus was clear. Not only in definition, but in pointing to action. "Store up for yourselves treasures in heaven" (Matt. 6:20). Make a choice against the immediate, against the gods of this world with their whining cries for refueling.

Choose relationship with the very Son of God. That's the treasure—Jesus Himself.

There is a price to pay, but there is everything to gain. Love costs; it cost God the sacrifice of His Son.

Sacrifice is almost an anachronism in our day. "You can have it all" is the slogan of our hedonistic, materialistic society. "Obey your thirst." Satisfy yourself. Take care of Number One. If it feels good, "just do it." Is it any wonder this culture has seen so many breakdowns in families and relationships?

But godly love can penetrate even the darkness of this world by the face of sacrifice. I know.

As Howard and I began moving in more honest dimensions in our home—learning to trust each other with our real selves, our feelings and our secrets—we found ourselves deferring to one another, not in a passive kind of way, but in an open, sacrificial way.

There were times we didn't want to be open and admit our feelings if they weren't "our best," but love calls for that kind of sacrifice, even when it's painful.

THE JOURNEY TO LOVE

There were—and still are—times when our comfort zones beckon us to self-protection to avoid conflict. But again, Jesus' love calls for a sacrifice of our own comfort. Thank goodness real people have a real Savior!

## Making the Honor Roll

I have always loved the honor roll of faithful pilgrims that appears in Hebrews, chapter 11. That stellar list inspires me to keep on my journey. People who gave their "all." By faith Abel, by faith Enoch, by faith Noah, Abraham and so on. To this day I am encouraged because of their love and faithfulness.

But there have been those in my life who have also enriched and blessed me with their love and faithfulness. You've met them in the pages of my story, seeing their real-life strengths and shortcomings. I have always loved my husband and my family, but for many years my own pain closed me to loving them freely enough to forgive their human failings. However, when Jesus heals our broken hearts, we see with new eyes of compassion and gratitude. We can truthfully honor them.

"Honor," according to Gary Smalley and John Trent, authors of The Gift of Honor, "is a decision we make to place high value, worth and importance on another person by viewing him or her as a priceless gift and granting him or her a position in our lives worthy of great respect; and love involves putting that decision into action."[8]

I invite you to join me in some moments of honoring these special people.

My dad.

I love looking through our scrapbooks and seeing pictures of him talking to Dr. Tozer or leading a choir. He has given me a rich heritage—everything from an appreciation of good music to an insatiable love of God's Word. He has left our family with a beautiful legacy of his love of music: a composition for each of his grandchildren. His sparkling eyes, his quick Irish wit, his heart for God. He's blessed my life beyond words.

My mom.

She was so easy to talk to. And she could be fun. From her I learned excellent homemaking skills—how to set a beautiful table, how to give a home the look and feeling of warmth, how to organize, how to make something out of little or nothing. She taught me manners, social graces, how to drive a car and play the piano. She is someone I miss to this day.

My husband.

Howard has experienced his own heart surgery. Determined to get further help, he went alone to counseling with Dick Williamson. He, too, faced the pain of seeing his flawed heart. To this day, he continues to learn how to walk openly and vulnerably with the Lord and others.

Howard has chosen to open his heart to God, to become filled with His love. Even at times when it was scary to him, foreign to his background, he has step by step taken his own journey to love. Like a mustard seed planted in his heart, faith has grown as the Lord promised. I honor the work of the Lord in him and appreciate deeply his love.

Our children.

In these past years with much of my time spent traveling, Jeff, Lisa and Scott have graciously accepted God's call on my life. I have felt their openhandedness, generously sprinkled with loving support. How I love and cherish each one. What joy they continue to give me. Truly, children are "the blessing of the Lord."

My brother, Jimmy.

My dearest childhood friend, Jimmy was so caring. He was the kind of brother who protected his little sister. He took me on wagon rides when I was little and to concerts when I was a teenager. Tragically killed at age 29, Jimmy had come back to the Lord and at the time of his death was studying for the ministry.

To this day I miss our warm, close relationship. But I am deeply grateful for those years we had together.

We are all products of the Fall. There is no perfect upbringing, no perfect family. But God always uses the broken places in our lives to "work for good." In my parents' later years, we enjoyed many evenings and Sunday afternoons of singing the old hymns, standing together around the piano. Of laughing over the dinner table. Of loving each other.

## When Love Moves In

When love moves in, watch out! Things change. Love has brightened our home—and our lives—with its powerful, healing dimension.

Sparring and arguing, being right and retreating. Anger, bitterness, hurt, pain—I knew this intimately for many years, as did Howard. But once you realize that your spouse and others do not hold the key to your life, that their response to you is not the evaluation of your worth, you become able to lay down your arms, your conditional acceptance and demands for perfect behavior. You are now free to receive what that person has to give you. Love has an open invitation to move in.

God did with us what He did for Joseph, sold into slavery by his brothers: He used what was meant for evil, for good. Out of our pain and hurt, out of our stubborn sinful strategies, He brought the healing power of His love and restoration. He wasted nothing.

I welcome you to look in on my life now:

I'm standing in a phone booth in an airport halfway across the United States on an Aglow trip. Lonely for Howard, I call between plane changes just to hear his voice. It comforts me.

It's after church, and Howard and I gather up Jeff and his family and head out for dinner. Now if there's fighting, it's over who gets to sit on Papa Howard's lap or snuggle in next to me.

It's early morning on the Edmonds waterfront. Howard and I

are walking along the beach, praying, talking, listening to the harbor wake up.

The surf's pounding in front of the condo on Maui. Laughing and splashing, we enjoy the surf together.

It's the Fourth of July, and the family and friends come for a potluck. Howard's barbecuing on the deck, the kids and grand-kids are splashing in the pool. Laughter rings out.

I've just come in from an overseas trip. Howard takes the bags to our room. I head for the kitchen. Flowers. He's filled a vase with red tulips and a few irises and arranged it on the table. It's a far cry from life in the little red house.

I drove by that place about a month ago. Alone in my car, I stopped for a few minutes, gazing at my "dream house." No longer red, no longer surrounded by immaculate flower beds. Shutters missing, fence needing repair, it looked tired and uncared for.

However, in my mind's eye I could still see that sparkling little house as it was the first day I laid eyes on it. Once more, I could recapture the overwhelming feeling of hope I had then. But it was hope misplaced. Hope that ultimately drained from me just as the water from Jeremiah's broken cisterns drained away.

There in front of the little red house, with the rays of the afternoon sun streaming across my car, I thought about the pain and anguish I'd experienced years ago. I thought about my long journey to love.

I didn't know then what I needed to know. That a love far, far beyond anything I'd ever known could be planted deep in my heart. That God's love would flower in "wasteful extravagance," filling me and sending its fragrance all around me.

# $\mathcal{E}$PILOGUE

I AM CONVINCED AND SURE OF THIS VERY
THING, THAT HE WHO BEGAN A GOOD WORK
IN YOU WILL CONTINUE UNTIL THE DAY OF
JESUS CHRIST [RIGHT UP TO THE TIME OF HIS
RETURN], DEVELOPING [THAT GOOD WORK]
AND PERFECTING AND BRINGING IT TO
FULL COMPLETION IN YOU.

PHILIPPIANS 1:6, *AMP.*

The Father has but one plan and purpose—to join His people to
Himself that we might come to know Him, become like Him and
express His life in the earth.

When we received Christ's death and resurrection, accepting
Him as our Savior, God joined us to Himself and infused us with
His own life. But that life must be developed, perfected and
brought to full completion. This God has promised to do. The

work He has begun in us He will faithfully continue throughout our lives as we look forward to the day of Christ's return.

As I look back on my journey to love, I can clearly see His hand at work—faithfully and continuously turning me from my self-centeredness, making me more and more alive to Him that He might express that life to those around me. But, as with any book written by a living author, my story does not end here. In fact, this was just the beginning of a whole new journey.

Free from the unhealthy self-absorption of my past, and with my new identity firmly established in God, I was able to enter into relationship with my husband on a whole new level. I began to understand God's purpose in putting man and woman together—what was really in God's heart when He brought forth the woman to be a "help" for the man's aloneness (see Gen. 2:18). God was able to teach me His design for marriage and family, an understanding that has radically altered our lives as Howard and I continue to grow together in our discovery of how God wants to be glorified in the earth through our union.

This subsequent journey unfolds in Fashioned for Intimacy, a book in which I explore how God is now seeking to reconcile men and women to one another—and to Himself—according to His original design.

God has a vital plan and purpose He intends to accomplish through man and woman, a plan that will yet come to pass before we see Jesus return for the Church. It is through this union—the marriage union and the union of male and female in the corporate Church—that God has always intended to accomplish His plans and to reveal His glory on the earth. It is only as we are set free from our own self-centered focus that we will have eyes to see His purpose and have a heart to enter into it.

# $\mathscr{E}$ N D N O T E S

## Introduction
1. Dr. Larry Crabb, *Inside Out* (Colorado Springs: NavPress, 1988), p. 25.
2. Ibid., p. 24.

## Chapter 2
1. David Seamands, *Healing of Damaged Emotions* (Wheaton, Illinois: Victor Books, 1981), p. 12.

## Chapter 4
1. A. W. Tozer, *The Pursuit of God* (Harrisburg, Pennsylvania: Christian Publications Inc., 1948), p. 11.

## Chapter 5
1. Larry Christianson, *Welcome, Holy Spirit* (Minneapolis: Augsburg Publishing House, 1987), p. 63.
2. Vincent Synan, *In the Latter Days* (Ann Arbor: Servant Books, 1984), p. 54.

## Chapter 6
1. Dr. Herbert Lockyer, *All the Women of the Bible* (Grand Rapids: Zondervan Publishers, 1988), p. 230.
2. Dr. Lester Sauvage, "Heart of Romance: Can a Billion Cards Be Wrong?" *The Seattle Times*, February 12, 1992.
3. Ibid.
4. Ibid.
5. Dr. Larry Crabb, Notes from Institute of Biblical Counseling Seminar.

## Chapter 7

1. William Barclay, *The Gospel of John* (Philadelphia: Westminster Press, 1975), p. 152.
2. Dr. Larry Crabb, *Inside Out* (Colorado Springs: NavPress, 1988), p. 26.
3. Ibid., p. 70.
4. Ibid.

## Chapter 8

1. A. W. Tozer, *The Best of A.W. Tozer* (Harrisburg, Pennsylvania: Christian Publications, Inc., 1978), p. 109.
2. Edith Schaeffer, "Keeping the Family Together," *Focus on the Family* (April 1984), p. 3.
3. Ibid.
4. David Seamands, *Healing for Damaged Emotions* (Wheaton, Illinois: Victor Books, 1981), p. 102.
5. Ibid.
6. Ibid., p. 103.
7. Tozer, p. 109.

## Chapter 9

1. Edith Schaeffer, "Keeping the Family Together," *Focus on the Family* (April 1984), p. 3.
2. Abigail Van Buren, "Dear Abby," *The Seattle Times*, April 26, 1992.
3. Catherine Marshall, *Something More* (New York: McGraw-Hill Book Company, 1974), p. 42.
4. *Spirit Filled Life Bible* (Nashville: Thomas Nelson Publishers, 1991), p. 179.
5. H. Norman Wright, *Always Daddy's Girl* (Ventura, California: Regal Books, 1989), p. 1.

## Chapter 11

1. Hannah Hurnard, *Hind's Feet on High Places* (London: The Olive Press, 1955), p. 15.
2. Ibid., pp. 15, 16.
3. Catherine Marshall, *Adventures in Prayer* (Old Tappan, New Jersey: Chosen Books, 1975), p. 22.
4. Paul E. Billheimer, *Don't Waste Your Sorrows* (Minneapolis: Bethany House Publishers, 1977), p. 88.
5. Ibid.
6. Joni Eareckson Tada, "Wasteful Love," *Moody Monthly* (February 1992), p. 32.
7. Ibid.
8. Gary Smalley and John Trent, *The Gift of Honor* (Nashville: Thomas Nelson Publishers, 1987), p. 16.

# What Is Aglow International?

—⁂—

*From one nation to 135 worldwide...*
*From one fellowship to over 3,300...*
*From 100 women to more than 2 million...*

Aglow International has experienced phenomenal growth since
its inception 30 years ago. In 1967, four women from the state
of Washington prayed for a way to reach out to other Christian
women in simple fellowship, free from denominational boundaries.

—⁂—

The first meeting held in Seattle, Washington, USA, drew more
than 100 women to a local hotel. From that modest beginning,
Aglow International has become one of the largest intercultural,
interdenominational women's organizations in the world.

—⁂—

Each month, Aglow touches the lives of an estimated two million women on six continents through local fellowship meetings, Bible studies, support groups, retreats, conferences and various outreaches. From the inner city to the upper echelons, from
the woman next door to the corporate executive, Aglow seeks to
minister to the felt needs of women around the world.

—⁂—

Christian women find Aglow a "safe place" to grow spiritually
and begin to discover and use the gifts, talents and abilities God
has given them. Aglow offers excellent leadership training and
varied opportunities to develop those leadership skills.

—⁂—

Undergirding the evangelistic thrust of the ministry is an emphasis on prayer, which has led to an active prayer network linking
six continents. The vast prayer power available through Aglow
women around the world is being used by God to influence
countless lives in families, communities, cities and nations.

# Aglow's Mission Statement

Our mission is to lead women to Jesus Christ and
provide opportunity for Christian women to grow in
their faith and minister to others.

—◊—

# Aglow's Continuing Focus...

- To reconcile woman to her womanhood as God
  designed. To strengthen and empower her to fulfill the
  unfolding plan of God as He brings restoration to the
  male/female relationship, which is the foundation of
  the home, the church and the community.
- To love women of all cultures with a special focus on
  Muslim women.
- To reach out to every strata of society, from inner
  cities to isolated outposts to our own neighborhoods,
  with very practical and tangible expressions of the
  love of Jesus.

—◊—

Gospel Light and Aglow International present an
important new series of Bible studies for use in small
groups. The Aglow Bible Study Series is now available
through Gospel Light. For information about these and
other outstanding Bible study resources from Aglow,
call Gospel Light at 1-800-4-GOSPEL.

# Aglow Ministers In.

Albania, Angola, Anguilla, Antigua, Argentina, Aruba, Australia, Austria, Bahamas, Barbados, Belgium, Belize, Benin, Bermuda, Bolivia, Botswana, Brazil, British Virgin Islands, Bulgaria, Burkina Faso, Cameroon, Canada, Cayman Islands, Chile, China, Colombia, Congo (Rep. of), Congo (Dem. Rep. of), Costa Rica, Côte d'Ivoire, Cuba, Curaçao, Czech Republic, Denmark, Djibouti, Dominica, Dominican Republic, Ecuador, Egypt, El Salvador, England, Equatorial Guinea, Estonia, Ethiopia, Faroe Islands, Fiji, Finland, France, Gabon, the Gambia, Germany, Ghana, Greece, Grenada, Guam, Guatemala, Guinea, Guyana, Haiti, Honduras, Hungary, Iceland, India, Indonesia, Ireland, Israel, Jamaica, Japan, Kazakstan, Kenya, Korea, Kyrgyzstan, Latvia, Malawi, Malaysia, Mali, Mauritius, Mexico, Fed. States of Micronesia, Mongolia, Montserrat, Mozambique, Myanmar, Nepal, Netherlands, Papua New Guinea, New Zealand, Nicaragua, Niger, Nigeria, Norway, Oman, Pakistan, Panama, Peru, Philippines, Portugal, Puerto Rico, Romania, Russia, Rwanda, Samoa (American), Samoa (Western), Scotland, Senegal, Sierra Leone, Singapore, South Africa, Spain, Sri Lanka, St. Kitts, St. Lucia, St. Maartan, St. Vincent, Sweden, Switzerland, Tajikistan, Tanzania, Thailand, Togo, Tonga, Trinidad/Tobago, Turks & Caicos Islands, Uganda, Ukraine, United States, U.S. Virgin Islands, Uruguay, Uzbekistan, Venezuela, Vietnam, Wales, Yugoslavia, Zambia, Zimbabwe.
*One extremely restricted 10/40 Window nation.

**How do I find my nearest Aglow Fellowship? Call or write us at:**

## AGLOW.
INTERNATIONAL

P.O. Box 1749, Edmonds, WA 98020-1749
Phone: (425) 775-7282 or 1-800-755-2456
Fax: (425) 778-9615   E-mail: aglow@aglow.org
Web site: http://www.aglow.org/